The Struggle for Economic Democracy in Sweden

GREGG M. OLSEN

Avebury
Aldershot · Brookfield USA · Hong Kong · Singapore · Sydney

© G. Olsen 1992

All rights reserved. No part of this publication may be reproduced, stored in a retrieval system, or transmitted in any form or by an means, electronic, mechanical, photocopying, recording, or otherwise without the prior permission of the publisher.

Published by
Avebury
Ashgate Publishing Limited
Gower House
Croft Road
Aldershot
Hants GU11 3HR
England

Ashgate Publishing Company
Old Post Road
Brookfield
Vermont 05036
USA

A CIP catalogue record for this book is available from the British Library and the US Library of Congress.

ISBN 1 85628 298 8

Printed and Bound in Great Britain by
Athenaeum Press Ltd., Newcastle upon Tyne.

Contents

Illustrations	vii
Acknowledgements	viii

1 Social democracy and the transition to socialism — 1
　On the limits of social democracy: the historical debate — 3
　On the limits of social democracy: the contemporary debate — 6
　The rise and fall of the Swedish wage-earner funds — 9
　Power resource theory and the historical development of Swedish working-class power — 14

2 The rise and stall of economic democracy in Sweden — 20
　Industrial democracy in Sweden — 24
　Economic democracy in Sweden — 31

3 Power resource theory and the strength of Swedish capital — 43
　The liberal era 1820-1932 — 49
　The social-democratic Keynesian era 1932-1976 — 53
　The crisis era 1976-1984 — 66
　Conclusion — 83

4	The ideological development of the SAP and disunity within the Swedish working class	90
	Party ideology and disunity in the Swedish "labour movement"	91
	Disunity within the Swedish working class	106
	Conclusion	112
5	Conclusion: The future of Swedish social democracy	115

Appendix: Swedish governments since 1902	122
References	124
Index	148

Illustrations

Tables

2.1 The spectrum of participation — 30
2.2 LO/SAP proposals for collective wage-earner funds: the three-step retreat — 39
3.1 The share of employment in the largest corporations compared to total manufacturing employment, 1983 — 72
3.2 The 20 largest Swedish multinationals — 76
3.3 Organization and unity of capital in Sweden — 85

Figures

2.1 The plan for economic democracy in Sweden — 23
2.2 Hierarchical range of workplace decisions — 31
3.1 The Wallenberg empire, 1984 — 73

Acknowledgements

The present work is based on doctoral research conducted in the Sociology Department at the University of Toronto. I am both fortunate and grateful to have had the opportunity to work with a distinguished group of friends and advisors on this study. A debt is owed to Robert Brym who, as supervisor of the study, was nothing short of exemplary, providing direction and unfailing support. I also benefitted from the involvement of Leo Panitch, whose incisive comments and critical questions sharpened the arguments in the thesis while his enthusiasm sustained my interest in the project. The advice and suggestions of the other members of the committee, Rune Åberg, Bernd Baldus and David Wolfe, were always most useful and very much appreciated.

Debts incurred during the research process, of course, reach far beyond the efforts of committee members. A no-doubt-incomplete listing of many others who offered encouragement and provided welcome comments on the manuscript (or parts thereof) would include Tom Bottomore, Joan Durrant, Lennart Erixon, Rianne Mahon, Rudolf Meidner, Ralph Miliband and Jonas Pontusson. As will be evident, a number of these academics were also among those whose work was indispensable to the project.

As a guest researcher at the Institute for Social Research in Stockholm (SOFI), I was provided with an ideal location to carry out portions of my research. I would like to express my appreciation to Rune Åberg, Henrik Tham and everyone else at SOFI for making my stay in Stockholm both enjoyable and productive and to the Arbetslivcentrum for opening its doors to me as well. I am particularly grateful to Bengt Åkermalm at the Arbetslivcentrum for his help in tracking down numerous and often obscure data sources and for his friendship. The knowledge, insight and generosity of researchers and officials, too numerous to mention by name, affiliated with various political parties (including SAP, Folkpartiet, Moderata Samlingspartiet and VPK), institutions and organizations (including Arbertslivcentrum, Fa-Rådet, IUI, LO, Metall, SACO/SR, SAF, SIF, ST, Statiska CentralByrån, and Trefond Invest) who submitted to lengthy interviews and discussions is gratefully acknowledged. The research trip to Sweden would not have been possible if not for the generous financial support I received from the Social Science and Humanities Research Council and from the University of Toronto.

An earlier and much shorter version of chapter three was published in *Studies in Political Economy* while another version of chapter four appears in *Regulating Labour: The State, Neo-Conservatism and Industrial Relations*. Dianne Bulback's much-appreciated word-processing skills and assistance with the demanding work involved in the preparation of the present manuscript were invaluable to its completion.

Finally, I once again owe an immeasurable debt to Joan Durrant. It is highly questionable whether I would have made it to this point without her love and unflinching support. It is to her that I dedicate this work.

For Joan Durrant

1 Social democracy and the transition to socialism

Introduction

A central concern within the political Left has been the viability of the social democratic vision of an "evolutionary" transition from capitalism to socialism. Neo-Marxists working within a structuralist and/or corporatist framework have tended to focus on the power and cohesion of capital, and have therefore emphasized the structural limits of social democracy. Those limits are its ironic but utter dependence, economically, on a robust capitalist economy and the concomitant need to "restrain" the working class. A number of these thinkers have also maintained that social democratic parties have been only interested in securing moderate reforms and "managing" the capitalist system from on high.

Marxian-inspired social democrats, alternatively, have tended to focus their attention on the "power resources" of labour. For them, increasing levels of working-class strength, measured by organizational and political power, have allowed the working class to obtain political democracy and "social" democracy, and will eventually result in the development of some form of economic democracy as well. From this perspective, the Swedish labour movement is significantly more powerful than its counterparts in other advanced capitalist nations. This is reflected in the existence in Sweden of a comprehensive welfare state, Marxian-oriented labour market policies, and more than forty years of almost uninterrupted power for the Socialdemokratiska Arbetarparti (SAP, the Social Democratic Labour Party).[1] Thus, it should come as no surprise that it was within the Swedish labour movement that a plan to foster economic democracy through the creation of an innovative form of "market socialism" was developed in the 1970s.[2]

This plan called for a gradual collectivization of ownership through the build-up of wage-earner investment funds and offered an imaginative alternative to traditional Left appeals for "more state," as well as to the market populism embraced by other Western nations in the latter part of the 1970s. However, from the time of its conception in 1974 to that of its implementation ten years later, the proposal underwent a series of modifications that greatly reduced its capacity to effect any meaningful change in socialist directions. The present study is centrally concerned with accounting for the demise of this original and very promising program to gradually democratize the Swedish economy. It will be argued here that, while power resource theory may address and better account for significant variations in labour movement' gains in advanced capitalist nations than other neo-Marxist approaches, it fails to provide an adequate account of the demise of the Swedish wage-earner fund plan. This failure largely results from neglecting to examine developments that increased the power of Swedish capital and to acknowledge sources of division, and hence, weakness within the Swedish working class.

Chapters three and four of the present volume attempt to take up this challenge. In chapter three it is argued that, whatever gains the Swedish working class made in increased power resources, changes in the organization and unity of capital in both the economic and political spheres, particularly over the past two decades, led to a much greater imbalance in power between labour and capital, in favour of the latter. Thus, an attempt is made to bring in traditional Marxist concerns with the strength of capital which have been largely ignored by power resource theorists. In chapter four, a critique is provided of power resource theory's over-estimation of the degree of unity and cohesion within the "labour movement." To this end, some of the divisions between and within labour's political and economic branches are identified by their commitment to economic democracy and their stand on the wage-earner fund question. The evolution of the official party ideology of the SAP is also examined here in an attempt to illustrate the SAP's changing position on the issue of economic democracy. However, before these issues and critical observations are dealt with, a discussion of historical and recent strategies to create industrial and economic democracy in Sweden, including a detailed description of the Meidner Plan and the diluted versions which followed, is presented in chapter two.

On the limits of social democracy: the historical debate

Attempts by social democratic governments to foster economic democracy and initiate a gradual, parliamentary and democratic evolution towards socialism -- through the creation of wage-earner funds as in Sweden or through the various other means adopted elsewhere -- have been, for the most part, unsuccessful. Whether or not such attempts are inevitably doomed to failure is a debate historically rooted in the late-nineteenth and early-twentieth centuries. Indeed, the Second International (1889-1914) had been largely concerned with "revisionism" and the question of "reform or revolution?".

The idea of reformism had "no distinct existence" in the work of Marx and was treated "ambiguously" by both Marx and Engels (Anderson, 1980; Kolakowski, 1985). Marx's commitment to class struggle as the means to overthrow a self-destructive capitalist system included supporting the proletarian struggle for democratic rights, the Factory Acts and other reforms, and he maintained that a peaceful rather than insurrectionary path to socialism was possible in some countries (the United States, the United Kingdom and the Netherlands) (Marx, 1977, 1978). And approval of some of the reformist tactics of social democracy, especially in Germany, can be found even in the unabridged version of Engels' well-known introduction to Marx's, *The Class Struggles in France* (Engels, 1978). Marx's theoretical ambiguity concerning reformism contributed to the flowering of a "golden age of Marxism" in which a number of competing interpretations emphasizing either a revolutionary or reformist path to socialism came to the fore. The most important interpretations were those of the revisionists, Eduard Bernstein and Karl Kautsky, and those of the revolutionists, Rosa Luxemburg and Lenin.

In 1891, the German Social Democratic Congress at Erfurt adopted a new program drafted jointly by Kautsky and Bernstein that attempted to overhaul the 1875 Gotha program that Marx had so severely criticized. While the first part, written by Kautsky, was a faithful recapitulation of Marxian theory, the section that Bernstein wrote dealt with practical objectives such as universal suffrage, a direct secret ballot, proportional representation, equal rights for women, progressive taxation, free medical care, freedom of speech and assembly, free legal aid, free schooling, the elimination of child labour, an eight-hour working day, the election of judges and magistrates, and the abolition of the death penalty.

Unlike Kautsky and other orthodox Marxists, Bernstein rejected Marx's labour theory of value and his "breakdown" theory of capitalist development. Through increasing concentration, monopolies and cartels, and the separation of ownership from control, the capitalist system was able to regulate itself and avoid crises. And there was no evidence of class polarization according to Bernstein either: the middle-class was not declining but growing, the working-class was not becoming increasingly impoverished but better off, and the ownership of capital was becoming more diffuse via joint-stock companies, not more concentrated. Bernstein maintained that, in light of these counter tendencies Marx had ignored, a gradual and peaceful evolution towards socialism through the adoption of parliamentary reforms was much more feasible than the revolutionary approach, for which the economic and social prerequisites had not materialized. For Bernstein, such reforms embodied socialism "if not in official form, at least in content" (quoted in McLellan, 1979:31). He stated that "there can be more socialism in a good factory law than in the nationalization of a whole group of factories" and that "'the final goal of socialism'...is nothing to me, the movement is everything" (*ibid.*). Bernstein's position, then, was not unlike that of the Fabians, whose work had influenced him while he was in Britain.

Critical of Bernstein's revisionism, Kautsky maintained an orthodox Marxist evaluation of social reality. He accepted both the labour theory of value and the inevitability of the collapse of capitalist society, the decline of which was evident in the end of free competition due to the development of cartels and monopolies. He argued that, despite increasing wages and better working conditions (which were the outcome of working-class unrest in any case), increased exploitation due to technological advancement meant that workers were relatively, if not absolutely, worse off. And the middle-class, while not necessarily numerically diminished yet, was on the verge of proletarianization. Stressing class conflict, Kautsky argued that the interests of capital and labour were irreconcilable and that piecemeal reforms alone were insufficient. However, in spite of his doctrinal purity, Kautsky is considered a revisionist because of his refusal to take any action (including advocating a mass strike) until a long list of preconditions were met, reflecting his commitment to parliamentary democracy rather than the dictatorship of the proletariat.

Rosa Luxemburg, the harshest critic of Bernstein's revisionism, also attacked his argument that capitalist development does not necessarily lead to economic collapse. To her, it was non-Marxist and fundamentally wrong. The extension of credit and cartelization were amplifying the inherent contradictions of capitalist society, not stabilizing it. And the middle classes, while not declining quantitatively, were forced to keep replenishing themselves as large capital recurringly mowed down small capital.

Emphasizing the necessity of the revolutionary movement to bring about socialism, Luxemburg (1982:25) maintained reforms were simply the "regulation" of capitalist exploitation. They were not an end in themselves, as Bernstein had argued. And their value lay not so much in their alleviation of miserable conditions but in the rehearsal for the decisive battle provided by the struggle for their achievement. Unlike Bernstein, she emphatically maintained that the state was not neutral, but a class state. The policies and reforms created by it and its democratic institutions would therefore always be in accord with the interests of the capitalist class and would be structured to reproduce the capitalist system. Thus, a "gradual revolution" or "socialism by degrees" was impossible. For Luxemburg,

> legislative reform and revolution are not different methods of historic development that can be picked out at pleasure from the counter of history,...[but rather]...are different factors in the development of class society. They condition and complement each other, and are at the same time reciprocally exclusive, as the north and south poles, the bourgeoisie and the proletariat (Luxemburg, 1982:49).

The chief proponent of the revolutionary or insurrectionary means of achieving socialism was Lenin. According to Lenin the achievement of socialism via the gradual build-up of parliamentary reforms could not possibly succeed for three reasons. First, open mass parties would fail to move in a socialist direction because workers are too economistic. Second, since real power does not reside in parliament, which is little more than a "talking shop," achieving a parliamentary majority would be an exercise in futility. And third, to transcend the capitalist system it was necessary to nurture the contradictions within it, not patch them up by means of reforms (Lenin, 1983, 1976, 1982). Having said this, Lenin's commitment to "insurrectionary politics" did not necessarily preclude parliamentary participation.

The current debate over the limits of social democracy and the path to socialism was set in motion by the turn-of-the-century reform-versus-revolution debate. The focus of the debate today is on the reasons for the apparent inability of contemporary social democratic parties to transcend social reformism -- even after lengthy terms in office.

On the limits of social democracy: the contemporary debate

Prior to World War I, social democracy was committed to "revolutionary reformism" or "reformist socialism." In the words of Miliband and Liebman (1986:476), it

> unambiguously stood for the wholesale transformation of the social order, from capitalism to socialism, on the basis of the social appropriation of the main means of production, distribution and exchange. This was to be achieved by way of a long series of economic, social, and political reforms, to be brought about by way of a parliamentary majority reflecting a preponderance of electoral and popular support.

Its rejection of Bernsteinian reformism was reflected in the adoption of an anti-revisionist resolution by the German Social Democratic Party (SPD) and the SPD-dominated Second International in 1903 and 1904, respectively. However, social democracy had begun an evolution toward "social reformism" as early as 1918 which accelerated after World War II. Initially stressing the type of social reforms espoused by the Fabians and Bernstein, which eventually led to the creation of the modern welfare state, the major European social democratic parties later also came to embrace Keynesian reflationary policies, the mixed economy, and the idea that public ownership was only the means to an end that might be otherwise achieved. In Sweden, the drift to social reformism was apparent in the SAP's rejection of the 1919 Gothenburg Program (a proposal drafted by Ernst Wigforss which was, in many ways, very similar to the Erfurt Program) as too radical, in the relatively low levels of nationalization, and in the notion of "functional socialism" which rested on the premise that the socialization of economic control, not ownership, was decisive.

In the late 1970s and early 1980s a "new political economy" emerged to challenge such pessimistic evaluations of social democracy in practice. Largely by means of quantitative, comparative studies, it suggested that social democratic and labour parties had achieved considerable success. Complementing the "structure versus agency" debate on the nature of the state, these studies set out to demonstrate that "politics matter," despite the contrary conclusions of structuralist or functionalist variants of neo-Marxist theories (Poulantzas, 1978b) or those of the "convergence," "logic of industrialism," and "end of ideology" theories that had been so popular in the previous decades (Cutright, 1965; Goldthorpe, 1964; Kerr et al., 1964; Lipset, 1983; Wilensky, 1975, 1976). They indicated that, in terms of a wide number of variables, including levels of unemployment and inflation

(Cameron, 1985; Hibbs, 1977), social mobility (Erikson et al., 1982), social equality (Åberg, Selén, and Tham, 1987; Björn, 1979; Dryzek, 1978; Hewitt, 1977; Leibfried, 1978; Stephens, 1980), gender equality (Ruggie, 1984), levels of public expenditure and the expansion of health and welfare programs, (Cameron, 1978, 1982; Castles, 1979; O'Connor, 1988, 1989), health and safety measures and worker participation in the workplace (Navarro, 1983; Stephens and Stephens, 1982), and "labour quiescence" (Brym, 1986; Cameron, 1985; Hibbs, 1976, 1978; Korpi and Shalev, 1979, 1980), social democratic governments have generally fared much better than their international liberal or conservative counterparts.[3]

Many Marxist critics, however, point out that social democratic governments have, despite proclamations to the contrary, been primarily concerned with managing the capitalist system -- giving it a more "human face" -- not transcending it, as Luxemburg had warned. For Miliband (1983:2), for example, these "moderate" reforms "represent no more than the partial humanization of an enduring system of domination and exploitation" which can be seen as strengthening rather than weakening the capitalist system by the "legitimating element" they bring to it. Proponents of the new political economy counter such attacks by arguing that the extent and nature of the reforms established in any particular capitalist country directly reflect the level of power attained by the working class. Once its power resources have increased, more far-reaching changes can be carried out. These changes can further strengthen labour's position by making it less dependent on market relationships (the decommodification of labour) and thus enabling it to enact further reforms that more directly challenge the capitalist system.

However, neo-Marxist critics maintain that the ability of social democracy both to improve the lot of and to decommodify labour -- primarily through the extension of the Keynesian-welfare state -- has been largely related to the existence of a number of conjunctural factors such as the elimination of unproductive capital during the Depression and World War II, the weakening of working-class organizations during the ensuing Cold War, the existence of large pools of cheap, skilled labour, the availability of new markets, an abundance of cheap raw materials, technological development encouraging productivity and consumer demand, and the creation of freer trade and a favourable environment under the economic and political hegemony of the United States, which produced higher investment ratios between 1950 and 1973 (Panitch, 1986b, 1986d; Wolfe, 1978; Wolfe, 1983). Once these special conditions had all been exhausted by the early 1970s, it appeared that the success of contemporary social democracy was largely dependent on constant economic growth and the profitability of capitalist enterprise. This was the primary contradiction of social democracy. And, it was held that these arguments applied no less to Swedish social democracy -- the most sustained and successful model of social democracy in the world to date -- however powerful the Swedish labour movement had become.

Despite its unrivalled success in achieving virtually full employment, relatively high wage levels, continued economic growth, rising productivity, and extensive welfare provision throughout the periods of post-war reconstruction (1945-1955) and full employment capitalism (1955-1973), the SAP was unable to prevent the Swedish economy from going into a tailspin like those of the other advanced capitalist nations in the 1970s and 1980s. Dramatic declines in Gross Domestic Product (GDP) growth (from a yearly average of 4.5 percent per year in the 1960s to 1.75 percent in the 1970s) and in industrial growth -- both "distinctly worse" than the Organization for Economic Cooperation and Development (OECD) average -- and an inflation rate "fairly close" to the OECD average bear this out (Jakobsson, 1986). Even Sweden's celebrated low levels of open unemployment deteriorated somewhat. However, at 3.5 percent Sweden's level remained much lower than the OECD average of approximately 10 percent for the 1970s. This was largely due to the existence of relief work, training programs, and other labour market measures, as well as heavy government subsidies to distressed industries and production for inventory (Jakobson, 1986; Olsen, 1988; Palme, 1975). After 44 years in power, electoral defeats for the SAP in 1976 and 1979 meant the full brunt of the international crisis, which was just beginning to impact on the Swedish economy, would have to be dealt with by a series of inexperienced "bourgeois" coalition governments over the next six years (1976-1982).[4]

While both public expenditure and marginal tax rates increased during the 1970s, findings of a number of studies suggest such increases were detrimental to economic growth and activity, preconditions for social democratic success. For example, Stuart (1981) argues that as much as 75 percent of growth rate decline in Sweden resulted from increased taxes. Similarly, Cameron maintains that the relatively higher levels of public spending in Sweden have contributed to a significant decline in the rate of capital formation. At approximately 60 percent of the GDP, "the public economy has approached, in size, relative to the entire economy, the...limits imposed by the fundamental requisites of the capitalist economy" (Cameron, 1982:61). According to Cameron, the plan for the creation of wage-earner funds in Sweden first and foremost reflected a concern to facilitate capital formation.

The rise and fall of the Swedish wage-earner funds

By the early 1970s, after more than two post-World War II decades of economic growth and prosperity, the onset of a severe and protracted international economic crisis had undermined the very foundations of "full employment capitalism." In Sweden, where the most visible signs of the crisis (industrial stagnation and higher levels of unemployment and inflation) did not really accelerate until the mid-1970s or later, the Left had already begun to abandon its "middle way" in favour of a "third way".[5] The so-called middle way between a capitalist market economy and Eastern European-style planned economies was a compromise between capital and a well-organized and politically cohesive labour movement, largely consisting of Keynesian macro-economic policies, a comprehensive Beveridge-style welfare state, Marxian-inspired labour market and wage policies, and relatively low levels of nationalization. While the form of welfare-state Keynesianism introduced in Sweden was, in many ways, much more successful than those employed in other countries, Sweden never progressed beyond "welfare capitalism." Welfare capitalist states are still marked by tensions between capital and labour, and political attempts to counteract inequalities produced by the capitalist economic system meet with varying but never complete success -- as seen previously with regard to the higher levels of public expenditure. Indeed, a number of the policies carried out by the Swedish social democrats in the middle of this century inadvertently created greater inequality and contributed to the crisis, setting the stage for the creation of a "third way" in the 1970s.

Reflecting both its Marxist heritage and its commitment to reformism, the SAP developed policies in the early post-war era that attempted both to accelerate the "maturation" of Swedish capitalism and to improve the conditions of the lower strata of the population, while simultaneously recognizing the centrality of capitalist economic growth. For example, the Saltsjöbaden procedure or Basic Agreement of 1938 between the LO (Landsorganisationen, the blue-collar Trade Union Confederation) and the SAF (Svenska Arbetsgivareföreningen, the Swedish Employers' Federation), which provided for an extension of union rights achieved in 1906 in exchange for the LO's continued acceptance of exclusive managerial control over decisions within the workplace (decisions concerning accelerated rationalization, technological change, assembly-line production and the use of time studies), was reaffirmed by the SAP after World War II because it promoted economic efficiency and growth (Korpi, 1978; Panitch, 1986d).

The cornerstone of the SAP's attempt to achieve economic stability and a more egalitarian distribution of income was the celebrated Rehn-Meidner plan, introduced in the 1950s and named after its principal developers, Gösta Rehn and Rudolf Meidner, two LO economists. Rather than conventional legislated wage freezes to control inflation, which benefitted capital while relegating unions to a passive role, they suggested a "solidaristic wage policy." Solidaristic wage bargaining required employers to pay equal wages for equal work irrespective of the profitability of the enterprise. This wage formulation process was later closely associated with the Scandinavian or "EFO" model, also named after its creators, Edgren, Faxén and Odhner, whereby wage increases would be linked to productivity growth and internationally-determined price increases.[6] According to Rehn and Meidner such a policy would achieve three desired goals: (1) the systematic elimination of the least efficient, least profitable firms unable to meet the demands of the solidaristic wage policy, leaving the more productive firms with a larger share of the profits for continued expansion; (2) the creation of wage equality and thus class identity and solidarity among workers; and (3) the promotion of voluntary wage restraint instead of a statutory incomes policy to control inflation under conditions of full employment.

Since it would also lead to massive layoffs as the less productive firms were weeded out, the solidaristic wage policy was complemented by an active labour market policy that allowed for the creation of a centralized labour market board (AMS, Arbetsmarknadsstyrelsen) to guide displaced workers into growth sectors or absorb them into retraining programs. In addition, the SAP introduced a superannuation system requiring both employers and employees to contribute to a state-administered fund, which was supposed to enable the SAP to more actively steer investments and thereby gain greater control over the economy.

These policies were not without negative repercussions. Dehumanization of work life and a lack of employee influence on the shop floor resulted from the continuation of the Basic Agreement. The active labour market policy led to regional imbalance. It depopulated Northern Sweden by socializing labour mobility to larger cities in the more prosperous South, creating a "center-periphery" problem by the 1960s -- to say nothing of the problems created by the psychological strain on those forced to move (Israel, 1974; von Otter, 1980).[7] And the solidaristic wage policy, implemented in 1956, not only led to further bureaucratization and centralization in the polity and central confederations, but also to an unprecedented concentration of wealth, ownership and power in the economy as successful enterprises prospered at the expense of unprofitable industry and industrial militancy. Firms with a capacity to pay higher wages collected "excess profits" and contributed to "wage drift" by paying their employees higher wages, thus undermining worker solidarity (Meidner, 1980a). In effect, the solidaristic wage policy was not even entirely successful in creating "socialism in one class." In the words of Rudolf Meidner (1980b:357) co-author of the policy, "the paradox arises that the structure of ownership takes on an increasingly disadvantageous character for employees, the more successful the trade unions are in their efforts to achieve parity of wages." Finally, decisions concerning reinvestment in Swedish industry were ultimately made by capital, despite the use of state pension funds to encourage and guide private investment, and the wage pressures created by the solidaristic wage policy left many capitalists unable or unwilling to reinvest.

By the late 1960s and early 1970s, amidst greater levels of inequality, a wave of unofficial strikes, and increasing unemployment and inflation, the LO recognized the urgency for the Left to abandon its middle way and develop a new third way; to move from social reformism toward reformist socialism. Having achieved political citizenship (universal suffrage) in 1918, and social citizenship through the extension of union rights in 1938 and welfare reforms, the LO now sought economic citizenship involving both industrial democracy (the expansion of employee decision-making rights at the enterprise level) and economic democracy (the collectivization of ownership and control).

The feasibility of wage earner funds as a solution to some of the immediate problems faced by labour and as a means of democratizing the economy had been discussed on a number of occasions in the past. However, at the 1971 Congress of the LO, a resolution was submitted by Åke Nilsson, the head of the Metalworkers' Union (Metallindustriarbetareförbundet), LO's most powerful federation, raising the question of wage-earner funds again. The motion to further study the question of wage-earner funds was adopted by the Congress, and Rudolf Meidner, a former chief economist with the LO, was asked by Arne Giejer, the LO Chair, to return from an academic post to head up the investigation. Meidner formed a working group, composed of himself and two assistants (Anna Hedborg and Gunnar Fond) and set out to develop a proposal that would complement the solidaristic wage policy and address some of the major problems of the day: democratic unaccountability in the economy, the increasing concentration of wealth and capital, and the inability of the capitalist system to ensure stable investment and employment.

Since the Meidner group was also concerned with the need for economic growth and the high rates of investment in industry required to sustain it, the idea of simply increasing company taxes was ruled out from the start. But the Meidner group did not want to develop a growth strategy which relied primarily upon wage restraint either. Instead, their program, which they presented to the LO Congress in 1975, called for collective capital formation through the creation of wage-earner investment funds. In short, the "Meidner Plan" suggested that each year 20 percent of the pre-tax profits of any large company (i.e., those firms employing over 50 or 100 workers -- accounting for two-thirds of all private employment) be transferred to an employee fund in the form of newly-issued stock shares which would be collectively owned and administered by the employees through directly-elected representatives. It was estimated that at the then-current rates of profit and growth, the more profitable firms would be employee-controlled within 20 to 30 years and the Swedish economy "essentially socialist" within 50 or 60 years (Himmelstrand, 1981; Korpi, 1978; Stephens, 1980, 1981). What was so innovative about the Meidner Plan, as Gösta Esping-Andersen points out, was that it seemed

> to satisfy two apparently contradictory goals: on the one hand, the pursuit of long-range profitability and high investment rates; on the other hand, a more equitable distribution of wealth, a gradual socialization of ownership, and the extension of worker representation in corporate management. In the short run, the plan would improve the companies' liquidity position and make more capital available for expansion and technological change. In the long run, employees would exercise majority control and enjoy the rights of ownership (Esping-Andersen, 1985a:298-299).

While various forms of traditional voluntary, company-linked profit-sharing systems date back at least as far as the early 1800s, the idea of mandatory, comprehensive and collective capital-sharing and capital-formation is relatively new. One of the first post-war schemes to redistribute wealth and increase employee influence over management-level decisions through the creation of collective "social funds" was developed in Germany in the late 1950s by Bruno Gleitze, a German union economist and head of a research institute (Wirtschaftswissenschaftliches Institut der Gewerkschaften). The "Gleitze Plan" suggested that all private firms over a certain size be legally obliged to contribute, in the form of shares, a specific percentage of their gross profits into social funds. The plan, for the most part, was adopted by the DGB (Deutscher Gerwerkschaftsbund, the German Trade Union Confederation) in 1968, and in 1972 the DGB endorsed a similar plan for such funds to counteract the increasing concentration in the German economy and to support their wage policies. However, this and various other proposals for economic democracy in Germany stalled amidst internal bickering within the coalition government (social democratic/liberal), disagreement within the DGB, and a deteriorating economy. Proposals put forward in the early 1970s by the LO and the Social Democratic Party in

Denmark to secure a more equal distribution of wealth and income as well as greater influence over the workplace for employees, met a similar fate.[8]

The German and Danish proposals, which Meidner and his co-workers studied carefully, had obviously had an impact on the shape of the Swedish wage-earner fund program. However, what made the Meidner Plan unique was its attempt to create solidarity within the working class by declaring that no personal benefit (individual dividends) from the collective capital would accrue to any wage earner/shareholder. Although the LO Congress did not endorse all of the technical details of the Meidner report, its four key principles were adopted in 1976:

> (1) The fund capital ought to be accumulated out of company profits. (2) The benefits of the scheme ought to accrue to all employees, whether or not they are employed by firms which contribute to the funds. (3) The fund capital should be built up by appropriations of "wage earner shares" corresponding to some portion of the annual profits. The capital may not be withdrawn from the firm, and, consequently, no individual is entitled to receive any part of the fund capital. (4) Since the proposed program is part of the LO's ongoing effort aimed at democratization of industry and codetermination of enterprise decision making, strong local employee influence was to be ensured by assigning a considerable part of the voting rights to local unions (Meidner, 1980a:166).

While the leadership of the SAP expressed general sympathy with some of the goals of the Meidner Plan, it did not come out in clear support of it and, mindful of the impending election, suggested a parliamentary commission to further investigate the proposal so as to delay taking a clear stand on the issue. Despite this precautionary tactic, the SAP was narrowly defeated in the 1976 election and replaced by a coalition composed of the three bourgeois parties. However, a series of scandals and the SAP's commitment to a limited build-up of nuclear power stations as a means to fostering economic growth, while decreasing Sweden's dependence on foreign sources of energy, were the main reasons the SAP lost power, not its qualified support for and willingness to study the feasibility of some type of wage-earner fund program.[9]

The SAP's tenure in opposition (1976-1982) was a period of intense struggle within and between the various political parties and labour market organizations. Of course the Meidner Plan was vociferously opposed by the most right-wing parties and organizations, but amendments or alternative wage-earner plans were proposed by almost all of the major political parties, organizations and private groups. During this period, Meidner's original plan was significantly diluted. The 1978 report prepared by a committee of SAP and LO members, entitled *Wage-Earner Funds and Capital Formation*, placed much more emphasis on economic growth, reflecting a concern with the continuing decline in productivity, which had begun in the early 1970s (Chandler & Trebilcock, 1986). This plan was not endorsed at the SAP Congress. It was not until 1981, after a number of additional amendments were made by a second LO-SAP committee, that a proposal was presented and accepted at both the LO and the SAP Congresses. In 1982 the SAP was returned to power and succeeded, although just barely, in legislating its wage-earner fund plan into existence the following year, but only after making further revisions. By this time, the Meidner Plan had been so watered-down that it was hardly recognizable. In this form, it would not democratize the economy and posed little challenge to capital.

Power resource theory and the historical development of Swedish working-class power

The past two decades have witnessed an outpouring of increasingly sophisticated analyses of the state in capitalist society, analyses largely written from a Marxist perspective or informed by Marxian categories and concepts. Perhaps one of the most fruitful of these approaches in terms of explanatory power has been the "power resource model" because it permits empirical evaluation of its hypotheses and assumptions. From this approach, the state is viewed not simply as an economically determined "shaper" of class struggle (uniting the factionalized capitalist class while fractionalizing the working class) but as an "arena" of class struggle, allowing for somewhat more independence between the economic and the political spheres. State policies and programs (as well as state structures themselves) are seen as both products and determinants of class struggle (Esping-Andersen et al., 1978). While acknowledging that the working class (i.e., all wage earners) is generally at a disadvantage with respect to power, the power resource approach also recognizes that the extent of that disadvantage can vary as the working class increases its power, thus contradicting central tenets of both pluralist and structuralist approaches. And, in direct contrast to theories of corporatism, which stress the state's role in the discipline, control, and integration of labour and the stabilization of the capitalist system, the power resource approach emphasizes that working-class power can be augmented and reinforced through the creation of social and economic policies geared to redistribution and prevention on a universalistic basis and the "decommodification" of labour (Korpi, 1985c; Esping-Andersen, 1987a).

Comparative studies invariably conclude that the Scandinavian countries obtain among the highest scores on various indicators of welfare effort and social equality. Sweden in particular, with its unrivalled comprehensive welfare state, celebrated solidaristic (wage-equalizing) wage policy, and highly successful labour adjustment policy, is often used as the standard of success. It should, then, come as no surprise that much of the pioneering, definitive and most influential work in this area has been carried out by what might be termed the "Scandinavian School" of neo-Marxist state theory. According to this growing body of literature, it is the power of the Swedish working class -- usually measured and defined in terms of organizational strength (trade union density, unity and centralization) as well as the stability and tenure of the social democratic government -- that is largely responsible for the creation and success of the Swedish model.[10]

A number of these studies describe how the Swedish working class has slowly but steadily altered the power structure to improve its position since the end of the last century, when the Swedish Social Democratic Party was founded in 1889. Late and rapid industrialization and a highly centralized export-oriented industrial sector led to the creation of industrial unions (rather than the non-centralised, economistic craft unions, which emerged during a "workshop stage") and their organization into a central confederation (LO) as early as 1898. As a result of its increased power resources, and the absence of ethnic, linguistic or religious cleavages within its ranks, labour was strong enough to gain the right to organize and bargain collectively through the "December Compromise" it reached with capital in 1906 -- albeit in exchange for exclusive managerial control over the organization of work, technological change and the hiring and firing of workers.[11] A dozen years later the labour movement succeeded in its quest for universal suffrage as well.

Increasing levels of unionization and the electoral victory of the social democrats in 1932 afforded labour the power to negotiate another settlement with the capitalist class in the late 1930s. Both anxious to avoid further legislative intervention, the SAF and the LO reached an "historic compromise," institutionalized in the 1938 Basic Agreement in the resort town of Saltsjöbaden near Stockholm.[12] The "Saltsjöbaden Agreement" blocked the demands within the capitalist class for legislation to curb trade union powers but, apart from the addition of some new minor restraints on dismissal and hiring powers, essentially reaffirmed management's exclusive control over decisions within the workplace. The agreement's collective bargaining and conflict resolution procedures reflected a large imbalance of power between capital and labour.

This new compromise, however, implied greater cooperation between the capitalist and working classes to increase the economic growth that both would benefit from. Strike activity thus declined to a very low level (Korpi and Shalev, 1980). The compromise also involved more limitations on the state's role in the economy. If it was tacitly understood that the working class would refrain from seeking state intervention to settle disputes in the labour market after 1938, it was more explicitly demonstrated in the late 1940s when the SAP abandoned its few remaining plans for nationalization and a planned economy. The labour movement was, however, free to further strengthen its position via more familiar measures which redistributed wealth (taxation, transfer payments, the solidaristic wage policy), ensured full or near-full employment (a variety of passive and, particularly, active labour market policies), and expanded the welfare state. Thus, although it had been forced to abandon its earlier more radical programs for a planned economy, Sweden's "Keynes plus Beveridge" formula of post-war statism is viewed by power resource theorists as a rational strategy for the working class given its level of power at that time.

By the late 1960s, however, the political and cultural climate in Sweden had become quite radical, perhaps best symbolized by the 1969 wildcat strike at the state-owned LKAB (Luosavaara-Kiirunavaara AB) iron mines in the northern town of Kiruna -- the first of a wave of illegal strikes of unprecedented magnitude. This radicalism was heightened by the reports of the 1965 Commission on Low Income and the 1968 Level of Living Survey, which surprised many when they concluded that inequality was increasing among large segments of the population despite the growth of the welfare state, and by the international economic crises of the 1970s and the subsequent decline in domestic industrial investment in favour of speculation or financial and foreign investments which endangered welfare programs and full employment (Broström, 1986; Erikson and Åberg, 1987; Higgins, 1986).

With near maximum levels of unionization among the blue collar (85 percent) and white collar (75 percent) workers, the close coordination of these unions in strong, if separate, confederations (LO and Tjänstemännens centralorganization, or TCO, respectively) and more than four decades of social democratic rule, proponents of the power resource model held that labour was finally ready to transcend its compromise with capital.[13] The capitalist system would finally be more directly challenged and transformed by the labour movement, as some of its central historical figures (Hjalmar Branting and Ernst Wigforss) had envisioned. Having achieved political and social democracy, it would now focus on the democratization of the economy as a whole. According to some proponents of the power resource approach, this was the third and final stage of a grand evolutionary scheme dating back to the early days of the SAP and the LO. It would be realized through the enactment of workplace legislation and the creation of wage-earner funds. However, notwithstanding the strength of Swedish labour, these offensives were to fall severely short of their goals -- an outcome for which power resource theory cannot account.

Notes

1. The Swedish Social Democratic Party took part in a coalition government with the Liberal Party in 1917 and was in power a number of times during the 1920s (1920, 1921-1923, 1924-1926). After its election in 1932, the SAP, apart from about 15 weeks during the summer of 1936, remained in power until 1976. However, it almost always had to rely on the support of another party to do so. (A list of Sweden's governments since 1902 is provided in the Appendix.)
2. Kuttner (1983:16) referred to the Swedish attempt to create a "wholly original form of market socialism." Market-socialist schemes can take a variety of forms, calling for various levels and types of socialized ownership, but all are reliant upon the market as a system of exchange rather than on some form of central planning. For a brief introduction to the idea of market socialism see Estrin and Le Grand (1989) and Yunker (1986).
3. Much of this literature contradicts earlier accounts which maintained that social democratic governments (in the Scandinavian countries) had largely failed to achieve substantially greater levels of social equality. See, for example, Castles (1975), Israel (1974), Parkin (1971) and Scase (1977). With regard to Sweden at least, this is because the greatest advances have been achieved in the past two decades. See Erikson and Åberg (1987).
4. Between 1976 and 1982, one or more of the three non-socialist or "bourgeois" parties (as they are often referred to in Sweden) held power.
5. Rudolf Meidner (1980b) used the term "third way" in reference to his plan for wage-earner funds because it sought to create a new type of economic system which would be quite different from either capitalism or "communism" (state control). He meant to distinguish development along such lines from traditional "middle way" strategies which are primarily concerned with extending the welfare state and pursuing

Keynesian policies within a capitalist system. There is some confusion over this term now because SAP's Finance Minister, Kjell-Olof Feldt (1987b:43), has referred to Sweden's third way "between excessive expansion and the excessive reduction in demand."

6. Simply put, the EFO model allowed economists to determine how much room there was in the economy for wage increases. The creators of the EFO model were the chief economists with TCO (Gösta Edgren), SAF (Karl-Olof Faxén), and the LO (Clas-Erik Odhner). A new model has recently been developed by Faxén, Odhner and the current chief economist with TCO, Roland Spånt -- the FOS model. See Faxén, Odhner and Spånt (1988).

7. Åberg (1987) has suggested that the geographic mobility encouraged by the Swedish labour market board was not quite as brutal as others have indicated. For example, the government not only assumed the financial responsibility of moving individuals and families to their new location but also made it possible for children to fly back home for free. In addition, it would pay for 40% of return costs if an employee was not happy in his new job at the end of one year.

8. For an account of similar programs and plans in other countries see Eidem and Öhman (1979), Gill (1984), Karlsson (1983), Öhman (1983), and Ramsay and Haworth (1984).

9. Much is often made of SAP's loss of power and Sweden's supposed electoral "swing to the right" in 1976, but it should be remembered that the social democrats actually lost less than 1 percent of their vote in 1976 -- four parliamentary seats.

10. See, for example, the work of Scandinavians such as Gösta Esping-Andersen, Walter Korpi, and also Ulf Himmelstrand et al. (1981), as well as that of Apple, Higgins and Wright (1981) and Stephens (1980).

11. The next few years, however, were marked by numerous strikes and lockouts. (One particular issue of contention involved the LO's insistence that the refusal of its members to work with strikebreakers was not a violation of the agreement.) This intense level of conflict between the LO and the SAF culminated in a general strike and lockout in 1909 and a disastrous defeat for the LO which lost over half of its members. The membership of the LO did not return to its 1909 level until eight years later.

12. Despite the fact that new legal restraints had been established in 1928 by the governing Conservative Party with the support of the Liberal Party -- making collective agreements legally binding and strikes and lockouts in disputes over the interpretation of such agreements illegal

-- the LO did not want to risk bringing down the minority SAP government by advocating the repeal of the 1928 legislation as had occurred twice in the 1920s. The SAF, for its part, was also nervous about further state intervention since the SAP was now in power, even if it was only a minority government. Although the SAP had denounced the legislation while out of office in the 1920s, it would not do anything to change it until the 1970s (Martin, 1977, 1979b).

13. While none of the power resource theorists maintained that a transition to some form of socialist society was inevitable, there was a common understanding that this was a very likely outcome given the dramatically improved power resources of labour. Ulf Himmelstrand (1981b:150), for example, stated that Sweden "is a country with enormous potential for qualitative and structural change, beyond the slowly incremental, and moving in the direction of socialist innovation within the framework of democracy." Apple, Higgins, and Wright (1981:298) reached a similar conclusion: "To mount a theoretically rigorous argument that Sweden is undergoing a long drawn-out transition to socialism would take at least a book in itself. We believe that such an argument can be mounted..." See also Korpi (1978b) and Stephens (1980).

2 The rise and stall of economic democracy in Sweden

According to the SAP's foremost ideologist, Ernst Wigforss, full democratization of the decision-making process in society must be a central component of any strategy to transcend capitalism and construct a viable socialism. This democratization would include public control of the economy at the macro level and a more democratic workplace at the micro level. Inspired by English Guild Socialism, his 1919 Gothenburg Program emphasized economic planning, worker co-determination, and an extension of consumer cooperatives as the means to gradually socialize the Swedish economy. Of course, the idea of introducing a measure of democracy to transform capitalism did not begin with Wigforss but can be traced back to nineteenth-century socialist doctrine.

Utopian socialists, such as Robert Owen and Charles Fourier (with their notions of autonomous communities based on industrial co-operatives and rural phalansteres respectively), anarchists, such as Pierre-Joseph Proudhon (with their conception of workers' associations), the revolutionary syndicalist movement in France (which called for an end to the capitalist state), as well as many left-wing social democrats and non-communist-party Marxists, envisioned some type of decentralized producer society rather than the centralised technocracy advocated by Saint Simon, and later by the Fabians, as an alternative to capitalism (Crick, 1987; Vanek, 1975). And, although Marx often refers to national or state ownership, he also maintained that the "national centralisation of the means of production [would] become the national basis of a society composed of *associations of free and equal producers,* carrying on the social business on a common and rational plan" (quoted in Elliot, 1987:297, emphasis added).

The world-wide radicalization of the late 1960s and early 1970s sparked a renewed enthusiasm and demand for democratic reform in the economy. Since then, the idea of somehow democratizing the economy, at either or both the micro and macro levels, has been justified on political, economic and moral grounds (Street, 1983). Political theorists, drawing on both liberal (John Stuart Mill) and democratic socialist (G.D.H. Cole) theories, argued that democracy in the workplace (as in other central institutions such as the family and the school) was necessary to ensure a fully democratic society. Carole Pateman (1970:42), for example, maintained that "the existence of representative institutions at [the] national level is not sufficient for democracy; for maximum participation by all the people at that level socialisation, or 'social training,' for democracy must take place in other spheres in order that the necessary individual attitudes and psychological qualities can be developed." For Pateman, then, a more democratic and participatory workplace is politically necessary to develop the worker's political education and democratic competence.

Drawing comparisons between the economic and political spheres, Robert Dahl (1984, 1985), the chief exponent of liberal pluralism, maintains that democracy is no less justified in the former sphere than in the latter. To avoid the concentration of ownership and power inevitable in capitalist economies, Dahl calls for an economy composed of worker-managed cooperative enterprises. This bears a close resemblance to market socialism. In a similar vein, Samuel Bowles and Herbert Gintis (1987) have pointed out the incompatibility of capitalism and democracy, of property rights and personal rights.

Studies indicating a strong positive correlation between labour productivity and worker involvement in decision-making have led to a call for economic democracy for primarily economic reasons (Hodgson, 1984). In particular, the Mondragon network of cooperatives in the Basque region of Spain, self-managed firms in Yugoslavia, and the success of, among others, the American plywood cooperatives in the Pacific Northwest, provided empirical evidence demonstrating the economic efficiency of such enterprises.[1] Worker-owned enterprises and self-management can lead to greater economic efficiency, according to supporters of these measures, because (1) employees are less concerned with short-run returns and are more willing to invest and make sacrifices to keep their firms from collapsing and preserve their jobs; (2) expenditure on enforcement and "guard labour" (surveillance, supervision and discipline) is much lower; (3) there is a larger pool of innovative ideas and opinions upon which to draw; and (4) a sense of community is engendered among employees. To encourage motivation and boost productivity, mitigate labour conflict, or attract and retain workers, capitalists have sometimes advocated that rank-and-file workers be given positions -- albeit minority positions -- in the ownership and control of their enterprises (Greenberg, 1986), leading to a healthy skepticism among many workers and their organizations regarding "worker participation," "employee involvement," or "quality of work life (QWL)" programs created by management.

Finally, others have argued that economic democracy is warranted from what may be viewed as a "moral" perspective. According to this view, employees have a right to co-determination in the workplace because they invest (and risk) their work and their lives in the production process, just as the capitalists risk capital through their investment (Broström, 1986). In addition, it is only a democratically-planned economy and worker-managed enterprises that can eliminate both the objective, structural roots of alienation and the subjective, psychological symptoms that accompany it. This would therefore promote creativity, job satisfaction and the development of human potential. Economic democracy is also viewed as a prerequisite for social equality. One prominent student in the field noted that "there is hardly a study in the entire literature which fails to demonstrate that satisfaction in work is enhanced or that other generally acknowledged beneficial consequences accrue from a genuine increase in workers' decision-making power"[2] (Blumberg, 1976:123). Some of the arguments for economic democracy cited above were not unfamiliar in Sweden. However, the Swedish labour movement, as noted in the previous chapter, was also confronted with specific and unique problems. For example, the concentration of wealth, ownership and power and the consequent undermining of the solidaristic wage policy all heightened its commitment to economic democracy.

A variety of proposals designed to engender a more democratic economy, in which people hold sway over both societal-level economic priorities and matters of immediate concern at work and in the community, have been set out by strategists on the Left over past decades. At the macro level they have called for the nationalization or socialization of the means of production (which in practice has left enterprises democratically unaccountable) and/or economic planning (involving, especially, public control over all decisions concerning investment and production, including capital formation, allocation of credit, and redistribution of wealth via wage, taxation and welfare policies).[3] Demands for micro-level democratization have similarly focused on the need for worker ownership (sometimes involving a broader vision of a society composed almost entirely of self-governing worker co-ops) and/or socio-technical changes and much more extensive legislative control over the workplace.

Since it is unlikely that workers within any single industry will fully identify with national interests or that public enterprises will provide workers with any more control in the workplace than private ones do, both micro- and macro-level changes are required. Like Ernst Wigforss' 1919 program, the Swedish labour movement's regenerated plan to democratize the economy recognized this need for democratization at both levels. Its plan for economic democracy, subsuming its strategy for industrial democracy, is summarized in Figure 2.1. While the latter would be approached through a "legislative offensive," the former was to be realised in the Meidner plan for wage-earner funds.

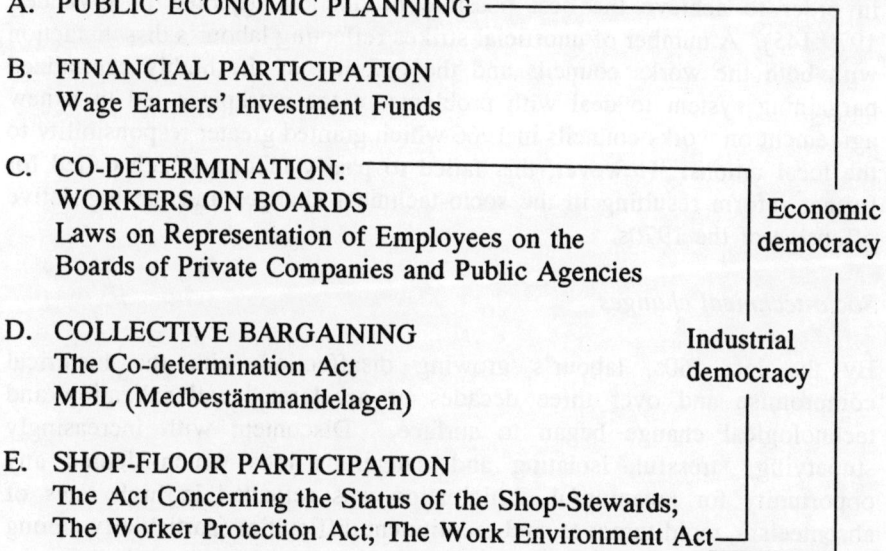

A. PUBLIC ECONOMIC PLANNING

B. FINANCIAL PARTICIPATION
Wage Earners' Investment Funds

C. CO-DETERMINATION:
WORKERS ON BOARDS
Laws on Representation of Employees on the
Boards of Private Companies and Public Agencies

Economic democracy

D. COLLECTIVE BARGAINING
The Co-determination Act
MBL (Medbestämmandelagen)

Industrial democracy

E. SHOP-FLOOR PARTICIPATION
The Act Concerning the Status of the Shop-Stewards;
The Worker Protection Act; The Work Environment Act

Source: Åsard, E. (1980). Employee participation in Sweden 1971-1979: The issue of economic democracy. *Economic and Industrial Democracy, 1,* 371-393.

Figure 2.1 The Plan for Economic Democracy in Sweden

Industrial democracy in Sweden

In Sweden during the early 1920s, the SAP had proposed the creation of enterprise committees composed of union and management representatives. However, afraid that both their autonomy from management and their claim to represent the workforce would be undermined, the unions were only moderately supportive of the proposal (Pontusson, 1986). In 1938, as noted earlier, management's exclusive control over all the important decisions in the workplace was enshrined in the infamous paragraph 32 of the Saltsjöbaden Agreement between labour and the SAF. This was a central component of the historical compromise. Thus, for the next few decades "industrial democracy" entailed little more than the creation of works councils composed of representatives of both labour and management in all enterprises with more than 50 employees. Built up through agreements between labour and the SAF in 1946, 1958 and 1966, they played an exclusively consultative role and had no real decision-making powers. The underlying purpose of such reforms, according to the LO-SAF agreement, was "to maintain continuous collaboration between employer and employee in order to achieve the best possible production" (quoted in Elvander, 1979:145). A number of unofficial strikes reflecting labour's dissatisfaction with both the works councils and the inability of the highly centralized bargaining system to deal with problems in the workplace led to a new agreement on works councils in 1966 which granted greater responsibility to the local unions. However, this failed to pacify labour, which called for further reform resulting in the socio-technical changes and the legislative offensive of the 1970s.

Socio-technical changes

By the late '60s, labour's growing disaffection with the historical compromise and over three decades of accelerated rationalization and technological change began to surface. Discontent with increasingly stupefying, stressful, isolating and dangerous jobs which denied any opportunity for meaningful participation was reflected in high rates of absenteeism, rapid turnover, and recruitment difficulties (particularly among the young). There was also an eruption of unofficial strike activity in the north, which quickly spread south to the industrial centres.[4] The effect of expressions of dissatisfaction on product quality, productivity, and profitability and the unfeasibility of continued reliance on immigration as a long-term solution, compelled management to address the question of industrial democracy more vigorously and directly (Holtback, 1988).[5]

Management was also motivated by an increasingly costly, inefficient and inflexible production process subject to breakdown and flow problems and inherently vulnerable to wildcat strikes. SAF's response to the growing demand for industrial democracy was embodied in the creation of a joint LO/SAF Development Council and in its "New Job Organisations" and "New Factories" projects. The response was aimed at increasing both profitability and job satisfaction through job restructuring and worker participation, confined within the limits of "self-managed" work groups and the joint consultative works councils.

The gradual dismantling of the old linear production methods (assembly lines, conveyor belts), which were based on Taylorist and Fordist principles, and the reorganization of the workplace, most conspicuous in the "experimental" Volvo-Kalmar factory which opened in 1974, went some considerable distance toward workplace humanization.[6] Although workers were still required to produce a certain set number of cars per hour, automated carriers, which transport vehicles to work stations and allow workers to tilt them 90 degrees, eliminated the dictates of the assembly line and the awkward, uncomfortable jobs formerly carried out beneath the vehicles. The creation of work teams, with rotating leaders and tasks, responsible for the production of entire systems (the electrical system, brakes, the driveline, etc.) and the consequent lengthening of the work cycle afforded the worker some new freedom and autonomy, and created more interesting work and a healthier work environment. And the "re-skilling" of workers necessitated by these changes has been accompanied by the employment of robots to carry out some of the most dangerous, dirty and repetitive tasks. With the onset of the global economic crisis of the 1970s and 1980s, and the intensification of international competition, the impetus for further socio-technical developments along these lines was provided. This is evident in the increasingly widespread use of multifunctional and reprogrammable robots, programmable controllers (PC), computerized numerical control machines (CNC), statistical process control techniques (SPC) and so on, and in the recent opening of a Volvo car plant in Uddevalla, where individual work teams build entire automobiles without direct personal supervision.

Although the socio-technical changes described above were clearly designed to eliminate or reduce micro and macro forms of worker resistance and improve the profitability of Swedish industry in the global market, it should be stressed that some of the changes made have rendered industrial work much more tolerable and would be prerequisites for worker satisfaction within worker-owned and worker-operated enterprises. However, there are conflicting tendencies in such developments. The creation of "independent" work teams with their own relatively noiseless, well-lit, well-defined work areas (at Volvo-Kalmar, for example, each team has its own building entrance, change room, coffee room and sauna) not only allows for the assimilation of absenteeism and the diffusion of collective concerns or expressions of dissatisfaction, but also fosters a level of competition and self-discipline which practically eliminates the need for supervision.

Similarly, automation may allow more freedom but, as Bengt Abrahamsson (1980:20) notes, "the concentration of information and monitoring capacities at central levels of the work organization lends itself easily to detailed planning and control of the conditions determining interaction at lower levels." More importantly, these socio-technical modifications do not address the original demand for workplace democracy at all. According to Winton Higgins (1986) the so-called "new factories" are largely the product of a management-directed revolution and signify a second stage of Taylorism, not a departure from it. While improving working conditions and engendering a feeling of independence and responsibility among workers, the hallmarks of scientific management -- separation of design and execution, managerial control over tasks performed, tools used, intensity of work, and so on -- remain firmly in place. One of the reasons these socio-technical reforms have not contributed significantly to the democratization of the workplace is that any negotiations between labour and management have always taken place over the introduction of new technology and new forms of work organization which have already been developed and adopted without any input from labour. By then, as Andrew Martin (1987b.108) notes,

> the scope for choice has been sharply narrowed. Therefore, these goals have to be pursued at much earlier stages. Unions must be able to influence not only the whole process of planning changes in production within the enterprise from the very beginning, but also the preceding R&D process by which the technological options that become available are themselves shaped. At the same time the exercise of such influence is recognized as a largely new function for unions, and one they are as yet poorly equipped to perform.

The legislative offensive

In light of the SAF's persistent resistance to labour's attempts to impinge on its right to manage the workplace via negotiations and collective bargaining, an increasingly radicalized trade union movement came to the conclusion that the limits of such traditional methods of labour-management relations had been reached. At its Congress in 1966, the LO appointed a committee to study the question of industrial democracy and prepare a report for its next Congress in 1971. Both the LO and the TCO, at their respective congresses in 1971 and 1970, approved the principle that industrial democracy be accorded the same status as wage and employment conditions in the work of labour organizations. The LO Report called for the replacement of "the existing regulations of paragraph 32 with a new labor law that would generate more symmetrical relations between capital and labor" (quoted in Albrecht, 1981:252-253) and was supported by the TCO as well as the Liberal and Centre parties. The Social Democratic government appointed committees of investigation (the Labour Law Commission), composed of representatives of the employer and union federations and the main political parties, and chaired by the former president of the TCO (Walter Åman). The committees were to propose amendments to the labour code that would foster greater equality between labour and management in the workplace. This led to the adoption of a series of legislative reforms which represented, according to Prime Minister Olof Palme, "the greatest diffusion of power and influence that has taken place in our land since the introduction of universal suffrage" and constituted a fundamental break with the terms of the historic compromise (quoted in Carnoy and Shearer, 1980:261).

Some of the most important laws passed during the 1970s and 1980s include the following:[7]

(1) The Act on Employee Representation on Boards (1973, 1976), which aims to give workers (in enterprises with over 100 employees) more insight and influence over their workplace by allowing them to elect two representatives to the boards of private corporations and public agencies. In 1976 these rights were expanded and allowed workers in companies of 25 employees or more to elect two members to the boards.

(2) The Job Security Act (1974), which regulates the hiring and firing of employees. It states that employers can only dismiss workers on "reasonable" grounds (for example, a shortage of work) and enforces priority rules based on seniority for grounded dismissals.

(3) The Promotion of Employment Act (1974), which obliges employers to give notice to the unions before dismissals and layoffs take place.

(4) The Shop Stewards Act (1974), which strengthens the positions of the shop stewards by guaranteeing their right to free time and paid time for union matters as well as other resources such as the space needed to carry out their activities.

(5) The Work Environment Act (1974, 1978), which sets outs basic rules concerning the physical and psychological work environment and allows workers, via majority representation on safety committees, to enforce protective measures through the imposition of fines or the closing of work sites pending state inspection.

(6) The Equality Act (1978, 1980) which aims to promote equal rights with regard to work, working conditions, and opportunities for self-fulfillment at work. It sets out rules regarding the prohibition of discrimination on the basis of sex and obliges employers to take active measures to promote equality.

(7) The most important law passed was the Co-determination Act (1976) or MBL (Medbestämmandelagen) which requires management to negotiate with labour for joint-determination rights in all matters concerning the hiring and firing of workers, the organization of work, or any other decision that would affect the workforce -- effectively nullifying paragraph 32. As a "frame" (or enabling) law, this Act leaves the working out of detailed regulations to central and local agreements but increases union access to company records and transfers the so-called priority of interpretation in cases of disagreement on the interpretation of collective agreement from the employer to the union (until the dispute is settled by the Labour Court).

While this legislation unquestionably improved working conditions for Swedish workers, as a means of democratizing the workplace it was ultimately a disappointment. Workers actually gained little leverage, for example, from having two members on company boards because employee board members are legally prevented from informing their unions about vital issues such as future shut-downs on the grounds that this could harm the enterprise. Moreover, the most important decisions are not made there but at higher levels by executives or anonymous financial groups (Gustafsson, 1986; Svensson, 1986). This is particularly true of companies owned by institutions and conglomerates.

Even the most far-reaching and comprehensive law, the Co-determination Act, does not apply to decisions made by conglomerates. And, where it does apply, it only requires employers to negotiate with workers before any decisions are made, not to follow the workers' suggestions. According to some cynical Swedish workers, this only means that employers now have to honk the horn before they run over workers. In addition, in certain respects, the co-determination legislation has served to protect capital and hinder worker solidarity: "By mandating consultation with, and approval by, employee representatives, the law built a buffer around potentially contentious issues between employees and management that greatly reduced the chance that the labour unrest of the late 1960s would reoccur" (Heclo and Madsen, 1987:124; also see Panitch, 1981) while "the union leaders' close cooperation with management weakened union members' confidence in their leadership, especially in situations involving cutbacks and rationalizations" (Svensson, 1986:293).

From the perspective of power resource theory, labour's ability to increase its influence in the workplace is dependent on the strength of the working class. Thus, it should come as no surprise that the Swedish working class has, through the enactment of workplace legislation, attained a considerable amount of influence in the workplace relative to its international counterparts. The extent of that influence, however, is dependent upon a variety of factors (Davies, 1979; Stephens and Stephens, 1982). The first factor concerns the degree of decision-making power transferred to the workers. This ranges from nominal forms of communication or joint consultation with management (where workers have little power) to co-determination (parity between workers and management) to worker control (where workers, as a majority, have more power than management) (see Table 2.1). The second factor pertains to the range of decisions over which labour has gained control or is able to influence. Ranked from the least to the most consequential, these include decisions over: (1) annual work and leave schedules; (2) work speed, work methods and choice of tools; (3) hiring, firing and the distribution of work tasks; (4) technology, organisation, planning and administrative routines; (5) choice, quantity and quality of products; and (6) distribution of profits, investments and financing (see Figure 2.2). The third factor involves the direction in which decisions can be influenced, i.e, whether labour is able to make positive decisions (raise issues and initiate decision-making processes) or only negative, defensive ones (dispute or veto management decisions). While highlighting the accomplishments of the Swedish workers in the workplace, a comparative study by Stephens and Stephens (1982:243) also noted that "the aggregate level of workers' control in no European country reaches codetermination. Co-determination occurs on the three lowest levels of the hierarchy of control in several countries, but on the upper levels the degree of control does not extend beyond joint consultation except in isolated industries in a few countries." With specific reference to Sweden, Hancock and Logue (1984:260) concur: "employee influence is virtually nonexistent at higher levels of company decisions affecting investments, product changes, new products, and the construction of plants abroad. The authority to initiate the latter type of decisions remains almost exclusively with management."

29

Table 2.1
The Spectrum of Participation

Degree of control by workers	Nature of worker involvement	General name
Greatest control or full industrial democracy	Ultimate authority rests with the workers themselves to whom management is responsible. The enterprise is also collectively owned by workers.	Workers' control or self-management
Lower limit of industrial democracy	Decisions made jointly by management or shareholder representatives (i.e., indirect participation) at board level or on works' councils.	Co-determination
	Workers initiate criticisms and make suggestions that are discussed with management. Management reserves the right to take the final decision but undertakes to provide workers with relevant information before such decisions are taken.	
Least control, lower limit of participation	Workers are informed of management decisions as well as the reasons for them.	Information/ communication

Source: Davies, R.J. (1979). Introduction: Industrial democracy in international perspective. In G. Sanderson and F. Stapenhurst (eds), *Industrial Democracy Today; A New Role for Labour*. Toronto: McGraw-Hill Ryerson.

- disribution of profits
- investments
- financing

- choice of products
- quality of products
- quantity of products

- technology
- organization
- planning
- administrative routines

- hiring
- firing
- distribution of work tasks
- individual-level decisions, such as work speed, work methods, choice of tools, ordering of tasks, etc.

- work and annual leave schedules
- administration of welfare services
- general collective decisions only marginally related to work

---

Source: Stephens, E.H., and Stephens, J.D. (1982). The labor movement, political power, and workers' participation in Western Europe. *Political Power and Social Theory, 3,* 215-249.

Figure 2.2 Hierarchical Range of Workplace Decisions

Economic democracy in Sweden

In the late 1960s and early 1970s, the SAP launched an "industrial policy offensive" in an attempt to extend public control over economic development. To this end, a number of institutions were established including the Ministry of Industry, the state-owned Investment Bank

(Investeringsbanken), boards for industrial and technological development, a holding company (Statsföretag) to co-ordinate the activities of state-owned firms, and the Fourth ATP Fund (a pension fund, see Chapter Three).[8] However, by the mid-1970s, Meidner and his research team at the LO had proposed a strategy to democratize the economy which would gradually transform the structure of ownership rather than rely solely on economic planning and hence fail to address directly the problems in organizational structure or traditional worker-management relations in the workplace.

A variety of proposals exist for the creation of a more democratic economy through changes in juridical ownership. The least far-reaching are those that simply advocate profit sharing. Popular in Britain and the United States, profit-sharing schemes have often been introduced in an attempt to quell labour unrest or as part of an anti-union drive. Apart from the economic insecurity that they engender and the fact it is virtually impossible for workers to determine what the actual profits of the company they work for are (because of executive expenses and so on), such plans do not provide for the sharing of power or control (Ramsay and Haworth, 1984). Thus, the Meidner research group steadfastly opposed the proposals for profit-sharing put forth by the Liberal party. In addition, it was felt that profit-sharing would threaten the solidaristic wage policy and undermine worker and union solidarity. Similar objections were voiced by Meidner and his colleagues at the LO in relation to individual employee stock ownership plans (ESOPs). Such plans are often created to provide corporations with low-interest loans, lower corporate income taxes, or unload unprofitable subsidiaries. Proposals for large-scale nationalisation were also rejected on the grounds this would lead to a concentration of bureaucratic power over workers (see Chapter Four), as were proposals for the creation of worker cooperatives. The latter, as islands of socialism in a sea of capitalism, would be constrained in terms of translating the democratic decisions of their members into market activities, and might also find it difficult to survive in a hostile capitalist environment (Pestoff, 1983). Moreover, workers in individual cooperative enterprises might simply pursue their own interests, weakening wage solidarity and creating divisions within the working class. While the Meidner group did not choose to adopt the above proposals, its plan for economic democracy through the creation of wage-earner funds was not entirely unlike them.

Swedish wage-earner funds and the three-step retreat

The idea of creating some type of fund to extend democratic control over the economy and foster greater economic equality has a long history in Sweden.

Ernst Wigforss had, as early as 1928, proposed setting up a "public investment fund" that would use capital obtained from an inheritance tax for various investment projects. SAP, however, shelved the plan after its electoral defeat the same year. At the 1951 LO congress, a branch of the municipal government employees union presented one of the first proposals for wage-earner funds in Sweden. It suggested that workers in the most profitable, highest-paying industries use their bargaining strength to achieve wage increases, a percentage of which would then be transferred to a "wage equalization fund" and used to supplement wages in the lower-paying sectors. This proposal was not adopted either because it amounted to a subsidization of inefficient sectors of the economy, which would contradict the tenets of the 1951 Rehn-Meidner plan emphasizing expansion, growth and structural rationalization. A decade later, at the 1961 LO Congress, a proposal for the creation of "branch rationalization funds" was put forward. According to this proposal, capital allocations obtained through collective bargaining would be used to facilitate expansion in the most efficient sectors of the economy. A similar proposal was also presented at the subsequent 1966 Congress, calling for the creation of "branch funds" that would be used to provide support for workers displaced by structural transformation in the economy. Neither of these proposals was adopted by the Swedish labour movement, which was more concerned with wage issues. Like the Meidner Plan, these proposals were both intended to promote capital formation without leading to a greater concentration of wealth or capital. But, unlike these proposals, the original Meidner Plan constituted a "non-reformist reform" because it would alter the ownership of the means of production and thus implied the transformation of Swedish capitalism. However, a series of changes made to the Plan in 1978, 1981, and particularly in 1983, undermined this potential. Consequently, the wage-earner fund plan, which was finally introduced by the SAP government in 1984, constituted another system-maintaining reform.

The original Meidner Plan 1975/1976[9] The first Meidner Report proposed a compulsory profit-sharing system. It called for a 20 percent annual levy on the pre-tax profits of every company employing over 50 workers (about 65 percent of all private employment) to be deposited into a central fund.[10] The profits would, however, be transferred to the central fund in the form of newly-issued shares rather than cash, while the capital itself would remain within the enterprise in which it was generated. The purpose of the central fund was simply to administer the allocation of the dividends the employee shares yielded. This task would have to be carried out by a central fund, rather than through numerous firm-based funds, if worker solidarity -- a major goal of the wage-earner fund program -- was to be promoted. While all union members would be responsible for the election of members to the board of the central fund, public representation would be excluded from the board and from involvement in this "domestic" matter. A system of sectoral funds (representing different sectors of industry) would also be created, however, which would have public representatives on their boards.

To ensure employees would have some control over their immediate workplace, rights to vote and appoint company board members on the basis of the fund shares obtained would accrue to the local unions until employee shareholdings in an enterprise represented 20 percent of its equity capital. In due time, when the 20 percent threshold was exceeded and the capacity to influence the economy had thus evolved beyond the enterprise level, the boards of sectorally-based funds would be responsible for filling the additional board places that employees were entitled to through subsequent share acquisitions. This would also prevent "group egoism" and attempts to exploit the public through collusion between employees and employers in individual companies. Until that time, these sectoral-fund boards would simply serve as consultative, advisory and supportive bodies to local unions and the Government. The members of the sectoral-fund boards would be appointed by both trade unions (within and outside the sectors in question) and public authorities.

The Report stressed that the shares were to be collectively owned, so that an individual employee would not be able to dispose of "his" or "her" shares. To ensure the availability of working capital for investment and prevent higher levels of inflationary consumption, the fund capital had to remain within the production circuit. Withdrawals of capital would only slow down the growth of the funds. Moreover, allowing workers to redeem individual shares would only undermine the principle of wage solidarity and frustrate the goal of altering the power structure and democratizing the economy.

The dividends earned on the shareholdings would also become the property of all wage earners rather than accrue to individual shareholders. Half of this income would be allocated to the sectoral funds and used to finance a variety of services, such as training to develop the necessary expertise for workers on the boards of companies, research in the field of work environment and other areas, and the provision of education, information and training for union members. All employees, including those working in sectors of the economy excluded from the fund system (small private companies, consumers' cooperative organizations, and public agencies and companies), would thus benefit from the wage-earner plan. The other half of the income from the shareholdings would be used to purchase more shares so that within 50 to 60 years, depending on the profitability of the large

Swedish firms, most of the Swedish economy would be "socialized." Of course, employees would enjoy influence much sooner as they slowly but surely gained a louder voice at shareholders' meetings, appointed more members to company boards and began to influence company policy. At its 1976 Congress, the LO overwhelmingly endorsed a new plan which, apart from its suggestion that all firms be included (even those with fewer than 50 employees) and its tempered anti-capitalist tone, was, in essence, the same proposal as the original.

The 1978 LO-SAP plan After the election in 1976, the SAP, now in opposition, began to work closely with the LO on questions concerning wage-earner funds. Cognizant of the major criticisms of the earlier plan made by Labour's traditional friends and opponents, a joint LO-SAP task force, headed by the LO's vice-chair, Rune Molin, presented a substantially altered plan at the 1978 SAP Congress. With levels of investment capital available for industrial expansion rapidly declining, the joint LO-SAP committee decided to set a fourth goal (alongside Meidner's original three) for the funds: they should "contribute to collective savings and capital formation for productive investments" (quoted in Hancock and Logue, 1984:263).

According to this new plan, only those firms employing over 500 workers (about 200 enterprises) would be required to contribute shares equivalent to 20 percent of their pre-tax profits to the fund. Dividend payments on employee shares would be included in this 20 percent contribution. And all such contributions would be tax-deductible, as would the dividends paid on shares owned by wage earners. Smaller firms could voluntarily participate in the wage-earner plan, but if they chose not to take part, they would be required to pay an amount equivalent to 1 percent of their payroll into a co-determination fund to promote wage restraint.

Instead of sectoral funds, the LO-SAP plan advocated the creation of 24 regional funds -- one for each of Sweden's 24 counties. The board members of these regional funds would be elected by all wage earners in the country. Local workers and these regional boards would now be equally responsible for voting rights and the right to appoint company board members until wage earner shareholdings in the company in question exceeded 40 percent. Thereafter, these responsibilities would accrue to the regional funds only. The administration of the shareholdings and the allocation of dividends would remain under the control of a central fund board.

In addition to this profit-sharing scheme, the LO-SAP plan called for the creation of a system of development funds. Separate from but coordinated with the wage-earner funds, these funds would be financed by a 3 percent payroll levy. The function of the development fund system -- composed of two central development funds (one to be controlled by wage earners, the other by representatives from the public at large) and 24 regional development funds -- was not to own firms. Rather, it would provide business and industry with the capital necessary for "extension, technical development, and innovation in production" through loans (quoted in Eidem and Öhman, 1979).

The LO-SAP's report represented a considerable compromise, particularly on the size of the companies which would be included and its proposal for a payroll levy, a suggestion Meidner had strongly opposed in his report. The SAP Congress supported the four goals put forth in the joint-committee report as well as the report's proposal for development funds, but did not endorse the plan itself. Rather, the Congress suggested that the issue of wage-earner funds be subject to further investigation.

The 1981 LO-SAP plan Amidst slowly climbing rates of unemployment, rising inflation, large budget and trade deficits, and low levels of investment, a new joint committee, chaired by the SAP's "shadow finance Minister," Kjell-Olof Feldt, presented its new proposal to both the LO and SAP Congresses in 1981. The economic crisis and, in particular, the need to generate a sufficient increase in investment capital, were the main concerns emphasized. A number of important modifications had been made in the new proposal. Eliminating the previous threshold on company size, this proposal scaled down the scope of profit-sharing by stating that companies would only have to share 20 percent of those portions of profits which exceeded a "normal" level (one or two million kronor for companies with one or two hundred employees respectively). The so-called normal level of profit would be determined in view of current rates of interest and inflation. In addition, companies would be allowed to make their contributions in the form of cash, thus requiring employee funds to purchase shares on the stock exchange. Moreover, the main source of financing for the wage-earner funds would no longer come from profit-sharing. Rather, it would come from a 1 percent increase in the payroll tax that was already levied to finance the pension insurance system. All companies, regardless of their size, would have to pay this levy. The money obtained from the payroll levies, profit-sharing and the dividends from shareholdings, would become part of the pension insurance system which would in turn allocate a major portion of it to the 24 regional funds, which could use it to purchase shares. There was also a minimum dividend requirement which had to be returned to the pension system to ensure that the boards of the funds purchased shares in the most efficient, profitable companies, rather than in declining industries in an attempt to save jobs.

The 1981 LO-SAP plan suggested two alternative proposals as to how the fund board would be appointed. The first called for the election of a general assembly in each of the 24 regions which would then select executive boards. Anyone with a stake in the pension system would be able to take part in these elections. The second proposal called for the Government to appoint board members from a list of nominees created by the unions and for board-representation from political bodies within the municipalities and counties as well. Voting rights associated with the employee shareholdings would be split evenly between the fund that acquired the shares and the employees in the company where the shares were acquired until the employees and the funds obtained 20 percent of the total number of votes in the company. Additional voting rights, which accompany additional shares, would go to the fund concerned. This modified plan was approved in principle by both the LO and SAP at their respective 1981 Congresses.

The 1983 wage-earner plan In 1983, a third task force, chaired by the LO's former research director, Per-Olof Edin, produced a final proposal for a wage-earner fund program which had been further diluted by additional amendments. As with previous proposals, this plan played down the idea of worker control and emphasized the need to increase the supply of risk capital for the benefit of both production and employment. Financing for this new wage-earner fund system would be basically the same as in the previous plan. It would come from a 20 percent profit tax on a well-defined calculation of "excess" profits (profits over 6 percent of the wage total or 500,000 Swedish kronor) and from higher payroll taxes on the pension funds (ATP) (now set at 0.2 percent). This would mean that approximately 2 billion SKr (Swedish kronor) would be paid into the fund system each year. Because of the specific construction of the plan, only about 10 percent of all Swedish companies would have to pay the levy on profits. Profit-sharing would not have to take the form of shares and companies would not be obliged to sell shares. And, as set out in the previous proposal, this wage-earner fund system was closely tied to the pension system and was obliged to return a real rate of profit of 3 percent to the ATP funds.

Instead of 24 regional funds, there would be a much less complicated system of five separate regionally-based funds administered by regional management boards.[11] The management boards were to be composed of nine members, five representing workers and four representing employers, to be appointed by the Government. Voting rights would accrue to the management boards. However, if a local union requested it, the board would be required to surrender the voting rights of half its shares in the company where the union was located.

In addition to these changes to the administrative aspects of the fund proposal, a number of more debilitating alterations were effected. First, each of the five funds would be allowed to hold a maximum of only 8 percent of the voting rights of any single firm. In addition, a law would be passed that would limit the total amount of voting power that could be attained by employees through their various funds to 49 percent. This would prevent the five funds from assuming control in an enterprise by combining their maximum level of voting rights (5 x 8 percent = 40 percent) with that of the Fourth ATP Pension Fund (10 percent). Of course the independent operation of each fund and its obligation to earn a secure return would militate against the likelihood of such a fund-coalition in any event. "And since most companies in Sweden are not listed on the stock exchange and have only one or two owners, even the extreme case of 49 percent fund ownership would not produce control of such companies" (Heclo and Madsen, 1987).

Second, it was now declared that the wage-earner fund plan was an experiment that would end in 1990. It has been calculated that, by this time, the five funds would have obtained only about 8 percent of the aggregate 1983 value of all the stocks on the Stockholm stock exchange. Prime Minister Olof Palme dealt the wage-earner fund plan one final blow when he assured parliament that there would be no new wage-earner fund programs after 1990. This plan would be *the* step toward democratizing the economy, not *a* step. According to Anna Hedborg, a senior economist and researcher with the LO, it was this declaration that took the dynamism from the fund system and made it irrelevant (Hedborg, 1987).

The final program for wage-earner funds, which went into operation in 1984, was a pale reflection of the original. (A summary of Meidner's original plan and the three successors is presented in Table 2.2.) Approaches that emphasize the increasing strength of the Swedish working class cannot explain why the latter's efforts to create economic democracy were thwarted in the 1980s. It is argued here that such power-resource approaches fail to consider the strength of capital (Chapter Three) and over-estimate the unity of the labour movement and its commitment to socialism (Chapter Four).

Table 2.2
LO/SAP Proposals for Collective Wage-Earner Funds: the Three-Step Retreat

	Meidner Plan 1975/76	LO-SAP Plan 1978
GOALS	(1) Support the Solidaristic Wage Policy. (2) Counteract the concentration of wealth. (3) Increase worker influence.	Addition of a 4th goal: the creation of investment capital.
FINANCING AND SCOPE OF THE PLAN	A 20 percent annual levy on the pre-tax profits of most/all companies in the form of newly-issued shares.	Only firms employing 500 or more pay the 20 percent levy. Payments and dividends are tax deductible.
ADMINISTRATION (type and number of funds, election to fund boards)	A Central Fund Board elected by union members. Sectoral Fund Boards with union and public representation.	24 Regional Funds elected by all workers. A System of Development Funds financed by a 3 percent payroll levy.
CONTROL (voting rights, election to company boards, use of dividends)	Local unions responsible for voting rights of first 20 percent of shares, Sectoral Fund responsible after this. Dividends used to buy shares and services.	Local unions and Regional Boards responsible for voting rights for first 40 percent of shares, Regional Boards for additional voting rights. Dividends as in previous plan.

Table 2.2 (continued)

	LO-SAP Plan 1981	SAP Plan 1983
GOALS	Emphasis on the 4th goal.	Emphasis on the 4th goal.
FINANCING AND SCOPE OF THE PLAN	A 20 percent annual levy on "excess" profits only. Main financial source is a 1 percent increase in the ATP tax.	A 20 percent levy on "excess" profits only. Firms are not required to sell shares.
ADMINISTRATION (type and number of funds, election to fund boards)	24 Regional Funds elected either by a general assembly or through Government appointments from a list provided by the unions.	5 Regional Funds with a worker majority. All 9 members appointed by the Government.
CONTROL (voting rights, election to company boards, use of dividends)	Local unions and Regional Boards responsible for voting rights for first 20 percent, Regional Boards for additional voting rights. Part of dividends go to ATP fund.	Voting rights to Fund Boards, but 50 percent can go to local unions. Part of dividends go to ATP fund.

Notes

1. And, as Robert Dahl (1985:131-132) notes, "producer co-operatives have usually been organized in the worst possible circumstances, when employees desperately attempt to rescue a collapsing company by taking it over -- often during a recession. It is hardly surprising that workers may fail to save a firm after management has failed. What is surprising is that workers' cooperatives have sometimes succeeded where private management has failed."
2. John Kelly (1988:218) is less optimistic with regard to levels of worker satisfaction: "The evidence on job satisfaction [is] more mixed with cases showing a variety of outcomes: long-term increases, short-term gains, no change, even long-term deterioration in a few cases."
3. Examples of recent strategies based on economic planning rather than nationalization or worker ownership include Carnoy and Shearer (1980) and Carnoy, Shearer and Rumberger (1983).
4. Rapid turnover in Swedish industries, as George Ritzer (1977) notes, was encouraged by benefit programs which allowed workers to change companies without losing any of their benefits.
5. Roger Holtback (1988), President and CEO of the Volvo Car Corporation, recently acknowledged these factors as the driving force behind Volvo's interest in introducing "worker participatory" schemes. Management had, for example, been severely restricted from hiring foreign workers by legislation passed in 1971 by the SAP at the LO's request (Ritzer, 1977).
6. The Volvo-Kalmar plant has received the most attention, but numerous other plants and industries in Sweden introduced similar changes -- for example, Volvo plants in Göteborg (Gothenburg), Lundwerken, Skövde, and Eskilstuna, and Saab-Scania plants in Trollhätten, Malmö and Södertälje.
7. For a more detailed description of this legislation see Gustafsson (1986), LO (1982a) and the Swedish Ministry of Labour (1985).
8. In addition, two government banks, the Postsparbank and the Kreditbank, merged in 1974 to form PK Banken. The State Enterprise Corporation (Statsföretag) was reorganised in the 1980s and renamed Procordia in 1984.
9. The descriptions of the various proposals for wage earner funds put forward by the LO and the SAP are based primarily on Albrecht and Deutsch (1981), Burkitt (1983), Eidem and Öhman (1979), Gill (1984), Gustafsson (1986), Heclo and Madsen (1987), Karlsson (1983), LO

(1976, 1982b), Meidner (1978), Ministry of Finance (1984), Rehn (1983), and Richardson (1982).
10. As Gösta Rehn (1983:8) explains, the Meidner plan advocated that the general 20 percent level be calculated before taxes to promote "the growth of capital for companies while reducing profitability from the point of view of the company owners. One intention of this construction was to invite workers to be cautious in their wage demands by offering them a part of the capital accumulated from increased profits. A growth-promoting profitability would thus be possible without provoking inflation."
11. Each of the five regional funds -- (1) Sydfonden (the South Fund), (2) Fond Väst (the West Fund), (3) Trefond Invest (the Third Fund), (4) Mellansvenska Löntagarfonden (the Middle Fund), and (5) Nordfonden (the North Fund) -- would receive up to 400 million SKr each year to invest in companies.

3 Power resource theory and the strength of Swedish capital

By focusing on variables that measure the strength of the working class, power resource theories represent a significant advance over other neo-Marxist accounts of the determinants of social and economic state policies insofar as they can explain the significant variation in gains achieved by labour in advanced capitalist nations. They can, for example, account for the extraordinary inroads made by the Swedish labour movement by pointing to the exceptional level of power resources it has slowly but steadily accumulated since the beginning of industrialization. However, despite the optimistic projections of its major proponents, the quest for economic democracy in Sweden was stopped short in the late 1970s and early 1980s and the Swedish working class was forced into retreat. Socio-technical changes and a "legislative offensive" aimed at micro-level democratization in the workplace were, ultimately, a disappointment, while a series of amendments to labour's macro-level program for democratizing economic life -- the plan for wage-earner investment funds -- left it practically stillborn, as illustrated in the previous chapter.

The failure of the power resource model to predict or account for this outcome is due in part to its apparent assumption of a necessarily zero-sum power relationship between capital and labour. This has resulted in an almost exclusive focus on the (seemingly) ever-increasing accumulation of power by the working class, while consequential developments, which can alter the overall configuration of power in society, have been largely overlooked. Any approach that purports to be describing a "balance" of power must, of course, not only examine the organization and power of labour, but that of capital as well. It is true, as Offe and Wiesenthal (1980:78) point out, that in any capitalist society capital will always have greater power and therefore a "superior ability to defend and reproduce power." However, that ability can be either augmented or diminished depending on a variety of factors, the power of labour being only one -- albeit an important one. Changes in the organization and unity of capital, in both the economic and political arenas, can tilt the balance of power more firmly in its own favour even if labour is simultaneously increasing its power resources, thus neutralizing these gains.

It will be argued here that changes in the organization and unity of capital, which took root earlier in the century, had significant implications for the configuration of power in Sweden by the latter part of the 1970s and early 1980s. An attempt will be made to complement the one-sided accounts provided by power resource theorists by tracing and examining the development of capital's power from the period of industrialization in the late-nineteenth century throughout the twentieth century. This will demonstrate that, following an extended period of dominance by capital (the Liberal Era), the working class was able to increase its power resources dramatically, which enabled it to demand certain types of concessions. During this period (the Social-Democratic Keynesian Era) labour reached an historic compromise with capital and recorded a number of important achievements. However, by the late 1970s (the Crisis Era) the balance of power began to shift back more firmly in capital's favour. Whatever its power within the context of Swedish capitalism, the working class was not sufficiently powerful to bring about the kind of system-transforming changes implied by the original wage-earner fund program. Rather, it was capital which was able to break with the historical compromise on its own terms. It is only by ignoring this development in Sweden that power resource theorists are able to present a steady, cumulative, "upwards and onwards" account of the power-building achievements of the Swedish working class.

According to Poulantzas (1978b:147), power "should be understood as the capacity of one or several classes to realize their specific interests." By definition, the power of capital is "privileged" in any capitalist society -- even where it has been somewhat bounded by over half a century of rule by a social democratic labour party, as in Sweden. The "difference" in power between capital and the working class can, however, be greatly increased depending on how capital is organized and how well it is unified in the economic and political arenas.[1] Five different indicators of the organization and unity of capital will be examined here: (1) the faction of capital that is dominant and the attendant overall growth strategy which it pursues; (2) the nature of the financial system; (3) the degree to which capital is internationalized; (4) the degree to which capital is concentrated and centralized; and (5) the orientation of key business associations.

The dominant faction of capital and growth strategy

Capitalist class unity in the economic arena is dependent upon the existence of a dominant faction of capital and its ability to develop an "accumulation strategy" or specific model of growth that advances the interests of and is acceptable to the non-dominant factions of capital while simultaneously securing its own long-term interests. While the acceptance of such a strategy does not eliminate conflict among the various factions of capital, it provides "a stable framework within which competition and conflicting interests can be fought out without disturbing the overall unity of the circuit of capital" (Jessop, 1983a:92). Of course the dominant faction of capital will not necessarily maintain its dominant position indefinitely. International economic and political factors beyond its control or influence may supplant it with another faction of capital, ushering in a new accumulation strategy, which will inevitably alter the balance of power between capital and labour.[2]

Of central concern here is the identification of either a *primarily* home-market-oriented faction of capital or a *primarily* export-oriented faction of capital as dominant in each of the three eras outlined above. The latter faction includes much of the "metalworking" or engineering sector, which began to take shape toward the end of the 1800s. The engineering sector is customarily divided into four distinct industries: (a) the fabrication of ferrous (iron) and non-ferrous metal products; (b) machinery (except electrical); (c) transport equipment; and (d) electrical machinery (Albinsson, 1967). L. M. Ericsson, the telecommunications manufacturer, is a good example of a primarily export-oriented industry. As early as the 1890s, it was already exporting over 80 percent of its equipment (Laxer, 1989). Home-market industries, alternatively, were closely tied to the domestic market because they (1) relied almost exclusively on domestic resources, (2) were largely dependent upon the domestic market to sell their products, even though many of them were also involved in exporting on a large scale, and (3) as highly labour-intensive industries, were extremely dependent upon the domestic labour force. Such industries include those involved in the production of raw materials, such as the ironworks, timber, stone, clay and glass industries, as well as those industries involved in construction, production of food and beverages or textiles.

Of course it should be emphasized that these two "orientations" (export-oriented/home-market oriented) were not mutually exclusive categories. As stated above, export industries did sell their products domestically and home-market industries were often heavily involved in exporting. Moreover, during the Social-Democratic Keynesian Era, many of the home-market industries became increasingly more export-oriented, both in terms of sales and production abroad. Automobile production, for example -- although part of the engineering sector -- was originally a primarily home-market industry and remained so throughout most of the Social-Democratic Keynesian Era. Even by the early 1950s, less than 10 percent of the production of passenger cars was being exported (Swedish Institute, 1984). However, during the latter part of this Era, in the 1960s and 1970s, automobile production became increasingly geared toward the export market. By the beginning of the Crisis Era the automobile industry was clearly an export-oriented industry. Other home-market industries, originally involved in the production of raw materials for the domestic market (as well as for export), became increasingly involved in the production of more sophisticated products for export, with mining companies and ironworks turning to the production of high-grade, specialty steels and tools; lumber and timber mills becoming involved in the production of pulp and paper and other forestry products; manufacturers of fertilizers beginning to produce pharmaceuticals, specialty chemicals, solvents and plastics. Partly as a reflection of such developments, as well as the growth and expansion of other industries within the engineering sector, export capital became increasingly important throughout the Social-Democratic Keyensian Era. By the 1970s, amidst the international economic crisis, it came to clearly dominate the Swedish economy, following over a century of almost uninterrupted dominance by home-market capital. This would have profound implications for the fate of the Meidner Plan and the viability of the "Swedish model" itself.

Type of financial system

The way the capital market is organized and the relationship that consequently prevails between the financial and industrial sectors of capital is also of great moment because it sets the boundaries the state must operate within -- regardless of the incumbency of a social democratic labour party. It thereby helps to determine which strategies and policies the state can pursue. Three distinct types of financial systems have recently been set out (Cox, 1986; Hall, 1984, 1986; Zysman, 1983).

In "capital market-based/industry-dominated systems," like those in Britain, Canada and the United States, the long-term funding required for industrial investment is obtained primarily through the securities (stocks and bonds) market and through retained earnings. Thus neither the banking institutions, which are geared to meeting industry's short-term needs, nor the state can exert any real control over investment and production decisions. Rather, such decisions are left largely to the industrial firms themselves.

In "credit-based/bank-dominated systems," like that of West Germany, a limited number of financial institutions provide the primary source of long-term credit for industrial investment -- the prices of which are set in the (oligopolistic) market. This allows them to significantly influence industrial decisions over investment and production and operate with little state intervention. To better assess the long-term growth potential of its clients, the financial institutions are compelled to develop a close working relationship with their managers and an interest in their affairs.

In the "credit-based/state-dominated systems," like those of France and Japan, industry is again largely dependent upon financial institutions for its long-term investment capital but the flow, prices and quantity of credit available are administered by the government rather than by the market. Here the government is a major player which, by manipulating the allocation and terms of credit, is able to strategically direct investment and production.

While only three basic models have been specified, it should be remembered that financial systems may fall somewhere between these ideal types and that they may change over time. Sweden's financial system seems to have fluctuated between the latter two models, with considerably more state control during the latter decades of the Social-Democratic Keynesian Era. However, developments that took place in the late 1970s and early 1980s led the state to play a much more limited role in the capital market, thereby decreasing the influence of the SAP and hence, the power of the working-class.

The internationalization of capital

The tendency for capital to increasingly engage in production for export and/or move production abroad also strengthens the voice of capital by rendering it less dependent on the domestic market and labour force and reduces the impact of the "gains" achieved by the domestic working class. Working class power resources, such as high levels of unionization or the incumbency of a social democratic labour party, lose a measure of significance when internationalization occurs on a large scale. While Sweden, as a small country, was export-oriented from the start and became increasingly so throughout the twentieth century, the internationalization of its economy increased dramatically in the 1970s and 1980s. This increase was concomitant with the rise of the export faction of capital and the new accumulation strategy.

Capital concentration and centralization

In a capitalist society, the structural "organization" of capital is vitally important. It occurs, originally, with the "'liquidation' of the means of production of small commodity producers" and is advanced through the continual merging of capital (Offe and Wiesenthal, 1980:74). Increasing levels of concentration not only centralize the economic power of capital but can help to unify further an already relatively small and cohesive group, reducing dissension by generating more congruent interests and concerns, thus making political organization and mobilization much easier. While the levels of concentration are high in any modern capitalist economy, Sweden's level surpasses even the highly concentrated economies of the United States, Great Britain and West Germany. This is owing not only to its open economy but to policies pursued by the social democrats which were meant to "hasten the 'maturation' of capitalist society" (Korpi, 1983:49). The strategy followed by the SAP to increase labour's power resources dramatically increased the power of capital as well by promoting extremely high levels of concentration.

Control over and orientation of employers' associations

In the political arena, unity among various factions of capital can be fostered through the creation of powerful, centralized employer and business associations, the efforts of which can play an important role in mobilizing public opinion. Such associations will, of course, usually serve primarily as an instrument of the dominant faction of capital. The extent to which the political parties on the Right are both united among themselves and affiliated with the employer associations and the various factions of capital will also affect capital's power vis-à-vis the working class. The centrality of these political factors was clearly indicated during the fierce struggles that took place in Sweden over the Social Democrats' proposals for a reflationary economic strategy in the 1930s, a planned economy in the 1940s, supplementary pension funds in the late 1950s, and wage-earner funds in the 1970s and 1980s. Of course, the degree of unity and cohesion within the capitalist class as a whole was also highly dependent upon the *nature* of the demands reflected in these various proposals. Thus both the proposal for a planned economy and that for wage-earner funds, which were the most threatening to Swedish capital, unified Swedish capital in its opposition. Regarding the less threatening proposals for Keyensian policies and supplementary pension funds, labour was able to strike a bargain with one faction of capital, thereby dividing capital to some extent.

The changing nature of the organization and power of Swedish capital along the five dimensions discussed above is examined in three broad eras: the Liberal Era (1820-1932), the Social-Democratic Keynesian Era (1932-1976) and the Crisis Era (1976-1984). By tracking the historical development of these indicators of the economic and political power of capital, a more balanced picture of the configuration of power in Sweden can be obtained and the modest beginning of an explanation for the arrest of economic democracy in the 1980s can be advanced.

The liberal era 1820-1932

The 1820s have been designated as the approximate time of inception of Sweden's relatively brief era of liberal or laissez-faire capitalism (Heckscher, 1954). Rapid economic expansion, however, did not begin in Sweden until the latter part of the nineteenth century -- a full 150 years after the disaster of the Great Northern War (1700-1721) and Sweden's fall from its position as a great power (1600-1720) into relative economic decline. It was, from the outset, both largely export-oriented, owing to a small domestic market and the absence of colonial outlets, and organized by financial capital. Indeed, even the considerable economic growth, which took place in the 1840s and 1850s (the "prelude" to industrialization), was in response to foreign (especially British) demand for agricultural resources and timber, and was financed by the newly-organized mortgage banks or merchant houses (Hörnell and Vahlne, 1986; Sandberg, 1978). While mortgage banks issued bonds abroad, particularly in France and Germany, to provide long-term loans to large Swedish landowners, merchant houses provided short-term credit to the nascent timber industry and arranged exports to foreign markets.

This economic activity, especially the export boom in timber, provided the ignition for industrialization in the 1870s. The construction of railway networks in the 1870s, an integral aspect of 19th-century industrialization, was also financed by the issue of bonds abroad by (or, in the case of government bonds, mediated through) Swedish financial institutions (mortgage banks, savings banks, commercial banks) while the emerging iron, glass and steel industries were financed through exporting merchant houses which were themselves dependent upon Dutch, English and German financial capital (Lash and Urry, 1987). However, by the 1890s, dramatically higher levels of bank deposits meant that this reliance on foreign capital could be greatly reduced and within a few decades Sweden would become a net exporter of capital (Laxer, 1981; Thunholm, 1981).[3]

During this era, the development of what were to become Sweden's three principal, privately-owned commercial banks occurred. Although they were initially primarily concerned with facilitating the importation of capital for the financing of railways, housing and municipal facilities, they increasingly provided the long-term loans that industries in late-industrializing countries like Sweden require to meet relatively high start-up costs. During the last three decades of the 1800s, the commercial banks assumed a central role in the financing of industry, while the state's involvement remained minimal.

If the Swedish banking system formally resembled Britain's, in practice it was much more like Germany's. As in Britain, Swedish banks were legally forbidden to issue or acquire the shares of client firms. However, by providing them with de facto long-term loans (and becoming heavily involved in their management) these "commercial" banks, like the German investment banks, played the central financial role during industrialization, rather than private risk capital or an organized capital market as in Britain or the United States.

The most influential of the three banks was Stockholm's Enskilda Bank. Established in 1856 by A. O. Wallenberg, founder of the Wallenberg financial-industrial dynasty, it both loaned capital to and invested in resource industries. With over-extended investments, the Enskilda Bank was brought close to insolvency during the economic crisis of the 1870s. However, by the 1890s it became even more heavily involved in industry, establishing or financing and restructuring existing industrial ventures, particularly in mechanical and electrical engineering, and investing in new and innovative products and methods of production or borrowing and refining foreign ones. The other two main banks were also engaged in similar activities at this time. Founded in 1871 by a group of former directors from the Enskilda Bank, Stockholms Handelsbank (SHB) became closely connected with Stockholm-based export industries while the Skandinaviska Bank (originally called Skandinaviska Kreditaktiebolaget) was primarily linked to the domestic-oriented industries.

This was the dawning of Swedish banks' extensive involvement in industry and the establishment of a significant number of what later became some of Sweden's world-leading export industries: Atlas Copco (1874), L. M. Ericsson (1876), Separator/Alfa-Laval (1878), ASEA (1883), SKF (1907),

Electrolux (1919) (Gustavson, 1986; Sweden Now, 1977). In the early decades of the twentieth century, the commercial banks (especially the Enskilda Bank) became even more involved in the creation, restructuring and takeover of industrial firms, despite legal restrictions on their deliberate acquisition of corporate shares. "The principle technique used to avoid such restrictions was the lending of money on the security of company shares, although holding companies, owned either by banks or persons 'closely associated' with the banks, were also used on occasion" (Sandberg, 1978:667). By 1911, even these obviously inadequate restrictions had been relaxed, allowing the banks to obtain shares more openly and directly, although such acquisitions were still subject to certain conditions. Thus, as early as 1925 the banks had become the largest shareholders in a number of the major mining, engineering and timber industries (Samuelson, 1957-58; Sandberg, 1978).

As a result of this economic activity, Sweden's Liberal Era witnessed the gradual formation of an export/manufacturing faction of capital largely engaged in engineering. However, this faction of capital was not dominant and would not be for some time yet. Despite the dynamic growth of the Swedish economy, the concentration and centralization of industrial capital did not really begin to take place on a large scale until after World War I in most branches of industry. This was particularly true of some of the export-oriented engineering industries. While a few branches of the engineering industry (especially electrical engineering) had become quite concentrated, this industry was still rather small, accounting for only 10 percent of all manufacturing production in 1912. The low levels of concentration in Swedish industry at this time resulted from the fact that they faced relatively little direct competition domestically (Lash and Urry, 1987; Montgomery, 1939). This meant that the export sector was still not very well organized or large and powerful enough to ensure that its own strategy for accumulation was dominant. Moreover, it must be remembered that at the turn of the century "agriculture still contributed more to the economy than all of manufacturing, including the engineering sector" (Laxer, 1989:93).

The organizational weakness of the export faction of capital was clearly evident during the economic crisis of 1873-1896 when the demands of a cross-class alliance of workers, farmers and the dynamic high-tech export industries and their financial allies for free trade were largely ignored. Protectionism prevailed for most of the period, as it did in Germany and France, reflecting the power of conservative forces linked to the aristocracy, the Crown and the Church as well as the wishes of the petty bourgeoisie, numerous small-scale farmers, and other vulnerable home-market manufacturers and their financial allies.[4] As Peter Gourevitch (1986:112) notes:

> the protectionists had the ample weight of the structure of interests on their side; they had all the advantages of special access and privileged information in the state; they had some organisational advantages; and they had the leverage provided by ideological resistance to market ideology.

The interests of export capital remained secondary and would be overridden by the home-market lobby and the Conservative Party again during the first decade-and-a-half of the twentieth century. The situation changed with the outbreak of World War I. The pro-German sentimentality of the conservative interests kept Sweden out of the war in 1914, leading to a blockade by the British and, consequently, a dramatic decline in exports. Export capital and its banking allies (the Wallenbergs in particular) thus encouraged the Liberal Party to ally itself temporarily with the Social Democrats in 1917 (around issues of free trade and universal suffrage) to overthrow the Conservative government of Hjalmar Hammarskjöld. When the conservatives were defeated three years later the door was open to an accumulation strategy based on laissez-faire policies and export faction demands for the balance of the Liberal Era (Apple, Higgins and Wright, 1981). The presence of division or unity among the bourgeois parties and the economic interests they represented would continue to play an important role in future struggles with SAP.

Sweden's liberal period also witnessed the birth of what would become its most important business associations. VF (Verkstadsföreningen), the association of engineering industries, was created in 1896, and SI (Sveriges Industriförbundet), the Swedish association of industries, was established in 1910 to produce and promote economic (and social) policy in general. SAF (Sveriges Arbetsgivareföreningen), the powerful central employers' confederation, was established in 1902. According to Geoffrey Ingham (1974), it emerged in response to high levels of industrial concentration in some sectors which provided the basis for employer solidarity. Others have focused on the stiff competition still existing in most sectors of the Swedish economy at that time, or on specific political catalysts. The latter include the creation of the LO in 1898 and the 1902 general strike and demonstration in support of the franchise, which involved approximately 120,000 people from a wide spectrum of political concerns (labour, temperance, liberal, and non-conformist church movements) (Fulcher, 1988a; Jackson and Sisson, 1976).

From the earliest years of its existence, SAF was a much more centralized federation than its counterpart, the LO. It had a level of authority and control over its numerous, mostly small-scale, members that the LO would not even approach for a number of decades. This was evident during the outbreak of conflict over union rights which culminated in the 1906 December Compromise -- a compromise that favoured capital and would, in effect, be preserved for the next 70 years -- and a major defeat for the LO in 1909, after which it lost over half its members. However, the enactment of the restrictive strike legislation proposed by SAF and the Conservative Party would have to wait until the latter part of the 1920s, when the Liberal Party's courting period with the SAP and the LO had ended and it returned to the (bourgeois) fold.

The Liberal Era in Sweden was a watershed in which the political and economic foundations of capital's power were being slowly transformed. The growing significance of exports, the consequent emergence of an export-manufacturing faction of capital intimately linked to financial capital, and the creation of political vehicles to organize the diverse interests of capital would all be of critical importance to the struggle over economic and industrial democracy which would take place in the 1970s and '80s. It was clearly not only the working class that was in the process of building up its power resources. Changing alliances and divisions among various classes and class factions, and between the political parties, would also continue to play a central role throughout the twentieth century.

The social-democratic Keynesian era 1932-1976

During the Social-Democratic Keynesian Era, labour significantly strengthened its position as the SAP, upon coming into office in 1932, became much more influential in the capital market and introduced innovative reforms, such as the Rehn-Meidner model, which greatly improved the lot of the working class. Of course these reforms also served the interests of the capitalist class and did not challenge the accumulation strategy of the dominant home-market faction. With the increasingly international orientation of the Swedish economy and the higher levels of concentration among the export industries during this era, export capital assumed a more central role. Although it was brought into the compromise reached between labour and home-market capital, export capital did not challenge the home-market accumulation strategy, upon which the compromise was based, as it would do in the 1970s.[5] The Social-Democratic Keynesian Era also witnessed three battles between capital and labour -- precursors to the "great wage-earner fund debate" -- in which the significance of political unity was clearly demonstrated.

The struggle over the Keynesian agenda: disunity on the right

The expansion of world trade in the 1920s meant that the export sector and its laissez-faire politics reigned supreme. Between 1923 and 1930, export volume grew by 70 percent while home-market capital, the labour movement, and the agricultural sector suffered the consequences of "sound finance" -- high levels of permanent unemployment, low wages, low demand, low prices and high interest rates -- which excluded the use of demand management to stabilize the business cycle (Apple, Higgins and Wright, 1981). However, the collapse of this fragile international order and the onslaught of the depression ushered in a new Keynesian era with the election of the SAP in 1932 and the eclipse of export capital and its economic liberalism.

During this "first stage" of Keynesianism, the SAP abandoned the obsession of the previous bourgeois governments with balanced budgets. Instead it proposed demand management and deficit financing to achieve full employment, although the government was rather slow in implementing its new approach. Now allied informally with the Agrarian Party rather than the Liberals (through the famous "cow trade" or "crisis agreement" of 1933, which SAP engineered by promising to increase rather than repeal the existing regressive agricultural import duties), the Social Democrats appeared to some segments on the Right to be very likely to remain in power for quite some time and would thus have little difficulty in implementing their reflationary strategy. This caused a dramatic split between the home-market and export factions of capital and their respective political allies. Home-market capital, once again in control of the SAF following the decline of export capital, opposed state "meddling" in the economy but was quite unwilling to risk challenging the parliamentary power of the new "Red/Green" alliance. As Winton Higgins (1985:227) notes, it "had a great deal to lose if it allowed itself to be led into a doctrinaire confrontation with the government and export capital's equally doctrinaire campaign to hobble unionism and force down wages". Thus, SAF proposed that capital abandon previous demands for further state regulation of trade union activity and negotiate with worker and farmer organizations directly in the labour market. There it could mobilize its natural superiority without state intervention. It was soon joined by VF and SI, two key employer associations, which had previously been calling for significant wage reductions as a central part of their depression programs. As a result of this strategy, SAF and its allies rejected any proposals for legislation aimed at limiting the workers' right to strike in the interests of "innocent" third parties, and were supported in this by the Conservative Party in 1935.

On the other side of the divide were the managing directors of five of the largest engineering/export industries, ASEA, Electrolux, L. M. Ericsson, Separator, and SKF, with their strong personal and financial links to the large commercial banks. The "Big Five" leaders (later to become six when the director of AGA joined in 1941) formed a pressure group called the Directors' Club in 1933. Under the leadership of Erik Österberg, it sought to persuade the leaders of the business community and the bourgeois parties to oppose the "economic authoritarianism" underlying the social democratic program and to mount an ideological campaign to unseat the new government and return to the liberalism of the 1920s. Export capital wished to lower wage costs in order to improve their international competitiveness As Peter Gourevitch (1986:133) suggests, "the various aspects of economic nationalism, such as domestic reflation, the boosting of internal demand, the protectionism, would do little good for big Swedish companies, because the home market was so small."

The determination of the home-market lobby to cooperate with the SAP, allied again with the Agrarian Party after the 1936 election, led to a resounding defeat for export capital and its ally, the dissent-ridden Liberal Party, and to the firm establishment of an accumulation strategy referred to by Jessop (1983a) as "social democratic Keynesianism." Its defeat was reflected in the 1938 Saltsjöbaden agreement, which strengthened the position of unions, and in the refusal of IUI (Industri Utredningsinstitut), a research institute created by SAF and SI, to engage in overt propaganda against the SAP's new economic program. Labour's success in pushing this program through depended not only upon its level of power (including its alliance with the Agrarian Party) as power resource theorists would have it, but also upon its ability to strike an accord with home-market capital and thereby encourage division within the capitalist class. However, when labour proposed more threatening measures, such as the post-war planning program, this strategy did not succeed.

The struggle over the post-war planning program: unity on the right

Other struggles took place over the next two decades which are also instructive for an understanding of the fate of the proposals for economic democracy in the 1970s and 1980s. This is particularly true of the bitter late-1940s struggle over SAP's post-war program for a planned economy, which in many ways parallels and foreshadows the battle over the wage-earner fund issue three decades later.

With the outbreak of war in 1939, and Sweden's consequent economic isolation from its major export and import markets, the Social Democratic government gave way to a national coalition government, which included the three bourgeois parties and representatives of capital in some key administrative posts. Nonetheless, SAP was able to direct economic activity via price controls, currency regulation, indicative planning, housing construction and control, and the creation of state enterprises, with little political opposition for most of the war. SAP's success in directing Sweden's war economy and its anticipation of another international depression following the war led to the creation of a post-war planning commission and the LO-SAP's post-war program, chaired by Gunnar Myrdal and Ernst Wigforss respectively. The post-war program called for extensive state planning.

Formally adopted in 1944, as the electoral popularity of the Communist Party momentarily increased, the "27 point program" had a familiar Keynesian ring to it, with full employment and the creation of a stable expansionary economy given top priority. It recognized the need to increase public control over investment and the allocation of credit, and called for the creation of a network of state commercial banks and the nationalization of insurance and credit institutions as well as the means of transportation and communication, natural resources and other industries, but only in cases where this was necessary to engender full employment and economic efficiency (Hancock, 1972; Lewin, 1975; Martin, 1985b). It was "planning and co-ordination," and not socialization, which was the major theme of the post-war program.

Nevertheless, the end of the war and the subsequent dissolution of the national coalition government unleashed a barrage of demands for the dismantling of SAP's war-time controls, regulations and institutions, and a sustained attack on the new proposal for further state penetration of the economy. Export capital, under the supervision of the Directors' Club, once again set out to persuade the bourgeois parties, home-market capital, and the employers' associations under the latter's control, to unite and mount a vigorous offensive against the SAP and its post-war program. Although home-market capital and the SAF were initially reluctant to end their cooperative relationship with SAP and feared a return to economic liberalism and domination by export capital reminiscent of the 1920s, the prospect of increased company, property and inheritance taxes, and the momentum of the offensive itself brought them on side.

Members of the post-war commission representing capital did everything in their power to water down and re-route the commission's recommendations, threatening to resign as a last resort. The IUI proposed schemes for the voluntary rationalization of industry, which would render the planning program redundant. Financial offerings were made by industry to the coffers of the bourgeois parties; most notable were the sizable contributions made by the export sector to the Liberal Party. The SAP also faced threats of capital flight abroad. In addition, a far-reaching propaganda campaign, PHM (Planhushållningsmotståndet or the Opposition to Economic Planning), was engineered. This involved press campaigns, public speeches and statements by prominent figures such as Ernst Wehtje, the president of the influential employers association, SI, and Herbert Tingsten, editor of the most widely-read newspaper in Sweden, *Dagens Nyheter* (a liberal daily), as well as the distribution of films, posters and pamphlets, and other efforts financed by private industry warning of an impending communist takeover.

Drawing heavily on the work of the Austrian economist, Friedrich A. Hayek, whose famous *The Road to Serfdom* made a lasting impression when it was translated into Swedish, the anti-planning offensive aimed to convince Swedes that the SAP's planning program would not only result in economic inefficiency but the loss of democracy, individual rights and even freedom of thought. The success of the propaganda offensive was evident in the 1948 elections to the lower house, when a plurality of the electorate supported the three bourgeois parties. Shortly thereafter, the SAP dropped its plans for nationalization, and other controversial parts of its program, but maintained power because the bourgeois alliance was unable to agree on an alternative program, and crumbled soon after its victory. The 1951 re-election of the SAP, and its entry into a formal coalition with the Agrarians, meant that home-market capital and SAF would return to the politics and tactics of the 1930s based on cooperation with the SAP and the LO. Once again the importance of division or unity within the capitalist class was clearly demonstrated. When fractured, capital (and its political allies) was unable to prevent the SAP from pushing its Keynesian program forward, but when unified, it discredited the SAP and extirpated its planning program.

Although the SAP could justify its retreat on grounds that the anticipated depression did not materialize, the sustained attack on the SAP's program and the increase in opposition strength in 1948 were instrumental in inducing the government to revise its policies' (Hancock, 1972). Writing in the 1960s, one prominent Swedish political scientist commented on the struggle over the planned economy: "Neither before nor since have ideological antagonisms been expressed with such force" (Lewin, 1975:290). Yet, less than a decade after this statement was made, another clash of the same magnitude was stirring. This struggle would be waged by the same unified bourgeois power configuration along the same ideological lines, using similar tactics, and with essentially the same outcome.

With the defeat of the post-war program, the establishment of another, more short-lived, SAP-Agrarian alliance (1951-57) -- once again preventing a unified bourgeois opposition in the political arena -- and a reconciliation between the Social Democrats and the bourgeoisie reminiscent of the 1930s, Sweden entered its "second stage" of social democratic Keynesianism. This period, Sweden's golden age of economic growth and prosperity, full employment and labour peace, witnessed an elaboration of the welfare state and the gradual implementation of the celebrated Rehn-Meidner model.

The Rehn-Meidner model

Although the Rehn-Meidner model embraced traditional labour movement goals such as full employment and wage solidarity, it clearly constituted a retreat from the ambitious planning program and a return to Keynesianism, albeit in a rather unconventional form. Expecting another recession like the one that followed World War I, the SAP was unprepared for the full-employment boom that emerged and attempted to deal with the spiralling inflation level by continuing wartime appeals for voluntary wage restraint in 1948 and 1949, while resuming its expansionary fiscal policies. Amidst high profits, dramatic price increases, and escalating wage settlements in different branches of the economy following the expiry of the wage freeze in 1951, the LO flatly rejected the SAP's plan for another round of wage restraint the following year. The LO maintained another incomes policy would further undermine the solidarity of the union movement and its relationship to the SAP. Instead, it urged the SAP to adopt the program presented to the LO congress in 1951, *Trade Unions and Full Employment* (LO, 1953), the classic expression of the Rehn-Meidner model.

First introduced in the late 1940s through a number of articles by Gösta Rehn and Rudolf Meidner, the model involved three interdependent components: (1) a solidaristic wage policy; (2) a restrictive fiscal policy; and (3) a selective labour market policy. These policy components were not entirely new but the way they were articulated and merged to deal with Sweden's postwar economic problems was innovative. While the Rehn-Meidner model both reflected and contributed to labour's increasing strength during the Social-Democratic Keynesian Era, it should not be seen as a threat or challenge to the market economy. Rather it was a means of restoring stability and promoting capitalist economic growth, indicating the superior strength of capital (under the leadership of home-market capital).

The hub of the Rehn-Meidner model was the solidaristic wage policy. Originally proposed by the Metal Workers' Union (Metallindustriarbetareförbundet, or Metall) in the 1920s, a relatively low-wage sector at that time, the principle of creating solidarity by reducing the gap between higher and lower paid workers became a widely held ideal by the 1940s.

However, the labour movement's previous concern with "egalitarianism" (a general reduction in wage differentials) gave way in the Rehn-Meidner model to an emphasis on "fairness" or pay equity (equal pay for equal work) in order to gain the workers' acceptance of wage differentials and prevent an inflationary "wage-wage" spiral under conditions of full employment (LO, 1953; Pontusson, 1986).

Later, the solidaristic wage policy's role in promoting structural change received greater emphasis. By requiring firms to pay "standard" wage rates, regardless of their ability to pay them, the solidaristic wage policy challenged the market allocation of wage increases. Workers would no longer subsidise inefficiency. Rather, inefficient firms would be forced to rationalize production or shut down while the most profitable firms would be encouraged to expand as a result of the restraint exercised by high-wage workers, culminating in higher average productivity and an increased scope for non-inflationary wage increases. However, as Jonas Pontusson (1987:484) points out, the solidaristic wage policy "promotes the restructuring of industry by *reinforcing* market-determined profit differentials. It speeds up the process of industrial change but does not alter the direction determined by market forces or corporate choices" (emphasis added). It should also be remembered that, although the LO leadership recognized the need for coordinated bargaining in order to implement the solidaristic wage policy, the institutionalization of centralized wage negotiations was initiated by the SAF and forced upon a reluctant LO in the 1950s (Fulcher, 1988a, 1988b). The significance of this fact would be demonstrated thirty years later when centralized bargaining fell into the SAF's disfavour.

Perhaps more important than the issue of solidarity was the labour movement's concern with maintaining full employment. To guarantee full employment even in the weakest sectors of the economy, conventional Keynesianism sought to create a very high level of aggregate demand. Rehn and Meidner argued that such an approach would result in excess demand, profit inflation and wage drift in the most dynamic, expanding sectors of the economy. This, they argued, would lead to an inflationary epidemic and, consequently, the need for wage and price controls. They rejected the general fiscal stimulants applied in the immediate post-war period in favour of a general restrictive fiscal (and monetary) policy. By reducing aggregate demand through the introduction of indirect (sales) taxation and other measures, and stimulating demand in particular localities only, inflation would be held in check and full employment maintained in the profitable sectors of the economy.

A restrictive fiscal policy would also prevent inefficient firms or sectors from increasing their prices to compensate for higher wage costs engendered by the solidaristic wage policy, since such increases would obstruct the structural changes the solidaristic wage policy was designed to facilitate. To ensure that the solidaristic wage policy was not offset by wage drift, fiscal policy would have to be sufficiently restrictive to squeeze the profit levels of even the most profitable firms as well. While this would lead to a decline in private savings, it would also result in an increase in public savings, which would be further supplemented by savings from a proposed public pension system (Martin, 1985a; Rehn, 1952).

Prevention of the inevitably high levels of frictional unemployment, which would result from the solidaristic wage policy and tighter fiscal polices, would require the use of selective labour market policies to encourage the flow of labour from declining sectors to expanding ones. Through the provision of job retraining, information and counselling, relocation incentives, and financial support, the labour movement's demand for full employment would be met. However, selective labour market policies would also serve the needs of capital by adjusting the labour supply to corporate investment choices and constitute a subsidization of recruitment and training costs (Pontusson, 1986).

Dependent as it was on parliamentary support from the Agrarian Party, the SAP was not really able to implement the Rehn-Meidner model until the 1960s. The Agrarian Party was strongly opposed to the re-introduction of indirect taxes and increased expenditures on labour market policies as well as a compulsory supplementary public pension plan. Thus, the second stage of Keynesianism was delayed and the SAP reverted back to fiscal policies designed to stabilize demand, such as the investment reserve fund system.[6]

A new role for the SAP in the capital market

As indicated previously, the organization of the Swedish capital market and the consequent relationship between industrial capital (both export and home-market), financial capital and the state in the Liberal Era closely resembled the "German model." As a late-industrializing country, Sweden, like Germany, became oriented toward heavy industry with high start-up costs. This led to the creation of a credit-based capital market dominated by a few commercial banks, (which had very close ties to industry and were able to operate relatively free of state control), and to an accumulation strategy based on the needs of home-market capital. With the election of the SAP and the onset of the Social-Democratic Keynesian Era, the capital market in Sweden became less "bank-dominated," but the monetary and credit policies which the SAP pursued did not challenge the prevailing accumulation strategy.

By the 1930s, the financial base for industrial expansion had broadened. Although still relatively undeveloped, the securities market and the insurance industry had been steadily expanding since the turn of the century. Moreover, the financial consolidation of industry, which had taken place in the 1920s, and the higher levels of profits it brought about, increased industry's reliance on self-financing and reduced its dependence on long-term bank loans to some degree (Pontusson, 1984b; Thunholm, 1981).

One year after the collapse of the Ivar Kreuger empire in 1932, the SAP enacted legislation that sought to protect the interests of the banks' depositors and shareholders by further reducing the involvement of the commercial banks in the affairs of the industrial sector. As a member of a Fabian research team studying Sweden shortly afterwards, Hugh Gaitskell (1939) enthusiastically endorsed this legislation as a "powerful instrument" that not only forbade banks from acquiring shares in industrial enterprises but also compelled them to concentrate on the provision of short-term credit. As in the Liberal Era, however, these new restrictions were easily circumvented. Through their holding companies (Investor and Providentia for the Enskilda Bank, Custos for Skandinaviska Banken, and Industrivärden for Handelsbanken) the commercial banks were able both to retain existing shares and to obtain new holdings, while much of the credit they provided continued to be of a de facto long-term character (Hufford, 1977; Pontusson, 1984b).

Neither the changes in the capital market nor the new legislation meant that the financial sector would cease to be closely involved in corporate affairs. However, the structural nature of the central bank in Sweden, the Riksbank, allowed the SAP, upon coming to power in 1932, to begin to play a much more active role in the credit market than the state had throughout the Liberal Era. Unlike in Germany, where the central bank (Deutsche Bundesbank) is autonomous from the federal government and is thus able to implement monetary and credit policies without its approval, the Riksbank is a formal agency of the Riksdag, the Swedish parliament.[7] The Riksdag exercises its authority over the Riksbank through a seven-member Board of Commissioners. Since all of the members of the Board are appointed by parliament (except the Chair, who is appointed by the government) and their terms of office coincide with those of parliament, monetary and credit policies depend on the distribution of seats in the Riksdag. The Board is formally responsible to parliament but, in practice, the Conservative, Liberal and Agrarian/Centre parties have had one Board-member/vote each, whereas the SAP has had three, excluding the Chair. While this does not mean the Riksbank simply acts at the behest of the government, it has ensured that it does not make any important decisions without first consulting the government, and does not act in opposition to the government's wishes. Of course, the Riksbank may have some influence on those wishes.

In the 1950s and 1960s, new regulations were introduced or tightened in the financial market which allowed the SAP, through the Riksbank, to enjoy considerable influence over monetary policy and the credit market in Sweden (Jonung, 1986; Martin, 1981; Skandinaviska Enskilda Banken, n.d.; Svenska Bankföreningen, 1987). This influence was exercised through the use of a wide array of instruments, including general and selective measures. The former included the discount rate (the cost to banks for borrowing from the Riksbank), open-market operations (the purchase or sale of government securities), and a cash reserve requirement (requiring banks to maintain a percentage of their deposits in accounts at the Riksbank), while the latter involved a liquidity ratio requirement (requiring banks to invest deposits in Government securities or housing bonds), lending regulations (or "recommendations" which limit amounts of lending), the regulation of securities issues and interest rates, and general and specific placement requirements. These measures enabled the Riksbank to closely control the volume, sectoral allocation and price of credit, make placement "recommendations" (which can be legally enforced), approve the issue of all bonds, and draw up banking policy.

Of course, as with fiscal policy, the SAP's use of monetary policy allowed it to realize some of its ambitions while still maintaining its historical compromise with capital, and without threatening the accumulation strategy of the dominant home-market faction. For example, by setting artificially low interest rates, backed up by currency regulations to prevent the flight of capital, the SAP ensured that cheap capital was available for industry. At the same time, this enabled the SAP to force private capital out of the housing sector so that affordable housing could be built, with public capital supplied from the pension funds and the state budget, by cooperative or public builders. The SAP/Riksbank has also obtained financing for its projects through the use of liquidity ratio requirements, which force banks to invest part of their deposits in government bonds, and through its ability to "shut out" its competitors in the bond market (Esping-Andersen, 1980a, 1985a; Martin, 1981). However, as Pontusson (1984b:41) notes, "regulation of the credit market has almost exclusively served as a means to channel credit for the finance of housing and public investment. The Central Bank has shunned selective intervention in the supply of credit to business." This reluctance on SAP/Riksbank's part to interfere with capital's investment decisions may have been more effective in discouraging capital flight than its monetary policy or exchange controls.

The pension dispute: disunity on the right

The dispute over the supplementary pension system reform (ATP, Allmän tilläggspension) of 1959, like the two struggles discussed earlier, indicates the pivotal role of political unity or disunity on the Right, and, in many respects, also parallels the heated conflict which erupted over the wage-earner fund issue almost two decades later. A trio of successive Royal Commissions in 1950, 1955 and 1957 had, predictably, failed to achieve consensus among members representing the major political parties and the leading interest groups. While they were all in agreement that the existing basic pension fund of 1913 was grossly inadequate, despite a large allowance increase in 1946, the deep ideological rifts of earlier (and later) encounters soon came to the fore, mirrored in the three alternative proposals for pension reform put forward.

Propelled by the LO, the SAP drew up a plan calling for a compulsory supplement to the basic pension amounting to 50 percent of the income earned by an employee during his or her fifteen best-paid years. It was to be paid by the employer into a fund that would be established and regulated by the government because conventional employer-run pension systems would be unable to provide comprehensive and standardized coverage and would hamper labour mobility by tying workers to their jobs (Pontusson, 1986). The fund was to be based on the "pay-as-you-go" principle whereby the fees paid by the employed finance the benefits of the retired. This would allow SAP immediately to provide considerably higher benefits and secure their value against inflation. These aspects of the plan reflected the SAP's continuing concern with "redistributive" or "consumption" politics.

Another central aspect of the SAP's plan was its recommendation that a large reserve be built up. This would not only guard against any sudden steep increase in pension payments and provide for a much larger population of future retirees, but, most importantly, provide a substantial source of public savings and thus complement the Rehn-Meidner model. The creation of a large reserve would be imperative because a public pension fund would further diminish the supply of private savings since workers would be less inclined to save for retirement while capital would be, at least formally, responsible for paying into the pension program. Employer responsibility for financing the fund would also help to control wage drift. The creation of a large pension fund would thus allow the SAP to enter the domain of "production politics" by providing it with a potential means of influence over investment.

Not surprisingly, capital and its representatives, SAF and the Conservative and Liberal parties, were vehemently opposed to almost every aspect of the

SAP program. While not as threatening as the planning program had been, they rejected the idea of a large extra-budgetary fund under state control. Instead, they proposed a strictly voluntary system in which benefit levels were determined via collective bargaining to ensure that they were related to economic performance and could be deducted from wages. Financing would be based on actuarial principles with the size of an employee's pension dependent on how much he or she saved and the rate of return on the savings (a premium reserve system) (Hadenius, 1985; Pontusson, 1986). Of course, the funds were to be administered by the employers. The Agrarian Party also put forward a proposal, calling for an increase in the basic pension rate and a voluntary supplementary pension system under government administration. Later, the Right was further fractured when the Liberal Party proposed a system of its own, which was very similar to SAP's but allowed individual employees to "opt out."

After a long, drawn-out ideological battle, a referendum, and the shattering of the coalition between the Agrarian Party (henceforth called the Centre Party) and the Social Democrats, the newly-elected SAP narrowly squeezed its pension program through when one Liberal member of parliament abstained from voting and broke the tie between the Left and Right blocs. The inability of the Right to unite around a common alternative to the SAP's collectivist pension plan had allowed SAP's victory, resulting in the creation of the "three" AP funds (actually one fund under the administration of three separate boards). However, capital's concern that the funds would be used for socialization or become a decisive instrument for determining the sectoral allocation of capital was soon allayed. Legally prevented from purchasing corporate stocks, the funds were restricted to indirect forms of lending to the private sector (through the purchase of bonds, promissory-note loans to intermediary credit institutions, retroverse loans through banks, and deferred debentures). These forms of lending provided negligible direct or indirect influence over the investment decisions of marketplace actors, despite the fact that the funds rapidly became a dominant source of capital in the credit market. This reflected both capital's superior power and the consequent willingness of the SAP to work within the boundaries of the historical compromise.

The concentration, centralisation and internationalisation of capital

The power of capital, particularly that of export capital, continued to escalate during the Social-Democratic Keynesian Era as the trends toward an increasingly export-oriented Swedish economy and the ever-higher levels of concentration which began in the Liberal Era proceeded apace. With the creation of the EEC (European Economic Community) in the late 1950s, Swedish industries rapidly increased their number of foreign operations within Common Market tariff walls to avoid disadvantageous duties and to allow them to compete more effectively. Subsidiaries were also established in North America and Latin America to circumvent tariff barriers, and in Portugal and Finland by the clothing industries to profit from the lower wages paid there. Between 1960 and 1965, foreign investments increased 80 percent and the total number of employees working in Swedish foreign operations grew four times faster than the growth rate of domestic employment (Berntson, 1979; Lash and Urry, 1987).

The third in a series of merger waves which have taken place since the turn of the century also occurred in the 1960s, dramatically raising the level of concentration in Swedish industry (Rydén, 1967, 1972). A well-known study carried out by C.H. Hermansson (1965, 1987) in the early 1960s documented the concentration of capital and the key position played by fifteen finance families that dominated the fifty largest industries and were closely linked with the three large commercial banks and the large insurance companies. A follow-up study carried out by an official commission (Koncentrationsutredningen) later in the decade confirmed the findings of the previous study, identifying seventeen powerful ownership groups; the fifteen families and two "bank investment companies," Industrivärden-Svenska Handelsbanken and Custos-Säfveån-Skandinaviska Banken, which were the second- and third-largest ownership groups, respectively, following the Wallenberg-Enskilda group (Commission on Industrial and Economic Concentration, 1976; Hermansson, 1987; Hufford, 1977). In addition to the increasing concentration of ownership, the study found a marked increase in the total proportion of workers employed in the 200 largest private sector companies from 1942 (25 percent) to 1964 (32 percent). The 100 largest industrial companies accounted for 43 percent of all employees in industry in 1964 and 46 percent of the total product of private industry. The authors of the study concluded "that the level of concentration in industry and commerce is considerable and that it has increased in the post-war era. The figures are, not surprisingly, higher than those for the United States and West Germany" (Commission on Industrial and Economic Concentration, 1976:31). Sweden's open economy has been cited as one of the major reasons for the high levels of concentration in the economy. However, as noted earlier, the solidaristic wage policy and the associated restrictive fiscal policies accelerated the tendencies toward concentration and centralization by eliminating those firms that could not pay the "standard rate" set for a particular industry. By the end of the 1960s, as a result of these twin trends toward internationalization and concentration, within both the home-market and export factions of capital, the Swedish economy became much more export-oriented. As Carl-Johan Bouveng (1967:48) notes, this general increase in foreign sales (and in production abroad) made it "increasingly difficult to distinguish between export and home-market industries." The onset of the international crisis in the 1970s would hasten this process by eliminating a number of home-market industries engaged in the production of raw materials.

The crisis era 1976-1984

According to Korpi and other proponents of the power resource approach, the legislative offensive in the workplace and the proposal for wage-earner funds in the 1970s signalled labour's willingness to transcend the historical compromise it had reached with capital in the 1930s and 1940s, when labour was just beginning to build up its power base. However, capital's success in arresting these radical ambitions indicates that, relative to capital, labour was not nearly as powerful as they had supposed. Rising levels of strike activity, the employer offensive against centralized bargaining and the solidaristic wage policy, deregulation and the SAP's ouster in 1976 after forty-four years in office, according to the very logic of the power resource model itself, suggest that the difference in power between labour and capital was widening in favour of capital. These developments must be viewed in the context of the global economic crisis of the 1970s and 1980s.

The exhaustion of the long post-war boom affected Sweden as it did the other advanced capitalist nations: declining profitability, productivity, and capitalization, sharply declining growth, escalating inflation, and higher levels of open or "hidden" unemployment. But the crisis also affected the Swedish economy in specific ways. First, a volatile and much less predictable international economy, (which resulted largely from the expansionary U.S. financing of the Vietnam War and which undercut the stability of the dollar and the international exchange rate on which it was based), made economic policy-making in Sweden much more difficult. For example, the calibration of centralized wage negotiations in accordance with the recently (late 1960s) formulated EFO model -- according to which the scope for wage increases was dependent upon price and productivity trends in the sectors of the Swedish economy exposed to foreign competition -- was rendered much more susceptible to consequential miscalculations (Heclo and Madsen, 1986).

Second, the accelerating demand for raw materials led to sharp price increases, which decisively turned the terms of trade against Sweden in the early 1970s. Sweden was hit particularly hard by the quadrupling of oil prices in 1973-74, since it was almost completely dependent upon oil imports to power its industries. Moreover, its large steel and ship-building industries were oriented toward the production of oil tankers and were thus severely crippled by the cutback in international oil trade. Third, the productivity growth which had been unleashed as a result of the solidaristic wage policy appeared to be exhausted. Finally, Sweden, as a world leader in high-tech industry, could no longer rely on borrowing and adapting foreign technologies as it had in the post-war period and was forced to compete with low-cost technology-copiers from Japan and parts of the Third World (Heclo and Madsen, 1986).

Through demand management, the SAP was able to delay the full impact of the international crisis on the Swedish economy. It pursued highly restrictive economic policies to "tunnel under" the global inflationary boom of the early 1970s and expansionary policies to "bridge over" the recession and maintain full employment in 1974. During this period, the SAP's minister of Finance, Gunnar Sträng, was internationally hailed as a "superman among finance ministers" (Erixon, 1985; Martin, 1981). However, the SAP was perhaps fortunate to have lost power in 1976 just as the Swedish economy began to reel under the full weight of the international crisis.

Although largely ignored by the Scandinavian power resource theorists, the crisis set in motion or accelerated developments which would significantly alter the configuration of power in Sweden. Changes in the financial market restricted the state's ability to manipulate monetary and credit policies as easily as it had previously done, allowing greater latitude for the financial sector. The decline of some home-market industries (accelerated by the oil shocks in 1973-74 and 1979, by intense international competition from the newly-industrializing countries, and by the internationalization of other home-market industries), ushered in an accumulation strategy organized around the needs of export capital, which had become much more concentrated and internationally-oriented in the 1970s and 1980s. By virtue of its control over SAF and its influence over other key business organizations, export capital was able to challenge the Swedish model and mount a unified opposition to eviscerate labour's program for wage-earner funds.

Deregulation and declining state influence in the capital market

Once in power, the three-party coalition (Conservative-Centre-Liberal) found itself suddenly accountable for a rapidly deteriorating Swedish economy.

After being shut out for almost half a century, it did not initially possess the confidence to tamper with the SAP's largely successful techniques for maintaining virtually full employment, or with its social programs, despite rhetoric to the contrary. In a desperate effort to hold down, or at least conceal, the increasing unemployment that the crisis had produced, the coalition actually expanded the SAP's labour market programs, increased the size of employment subsidies, and, in contradistinction to the Rehn-Meidner model, provided large grants and loans to failing firms. This proved to be extraordinarily costly. The central government's budget deficit, at only 2 percent of the GDP when the coalition was elected in 1976, had climbed to 13 percent by 1982 when SAP was returned to office (The Economist, March, 1987). At the same time "the current account balance with other countries fell from a surplus equal to 2.7 percent of the national income in 1973 to a deficit of 3.7 percent in 1982" (Bosworth and Lawrence, 1987:23). As a result of these twin deficits, Sweden became much more closely linked to the international financial market, significantly curtailing the influence previously enjoyed by the state over exchange control and monetary and credit policy.

Throughout the Social-Democratic Keynesian Era, the SAP-dominated Riksbank (through its Exchange Control Board) had maintained strict exchange control regulations which, by severely restricting the possibility for capital movement across national borders, shielded the Swedish credit market from foreign markets (OECD, 1981, 1982; Myhrman and Sundberg, 1986).[8] This allowed SAP to pursue counter-cyclical monetary policies geared to internal economic needs and ensured that the numerous regulations rationing the supply of credit in Sweden were binding. However, this autonomy was "dramatically reduced" in the late 1970s and early 1980s as Sweden's huge current account deficit forced the bourgeois government to seek financing abroad to offset the growing outflow of capital and hold down a rising inflation rate. This fact was recently acknowledged by Sweden's largest bank, which routinely publishes articles in its journal decrying the existence of strict regulations in the Swedish financial market (Skandinaviska Enskilda Banken, n.d.). Foreign exchange policy, while still strict by international standards, was eased to stimulate capital inflow. The Riksbank has also been compelled to adjust its short-term interest rate in close correlation with international rates to maintain a balance in its capital account. And, in contrast to all previous recessions since the post-war period, the state has been forced to abandon counter-cyclical policy in favour of a persistently restrictive monetary policy (Aspman and Lundberg, 1985).

The international trend towards deregulation has by no means left Sweden behind (Jonung, 1986; Myhrman and Sundberg, 1986). Between 1974 and

1985, no less than thirteen controls have been lifted (including the abolition of liquidity quotas and the liberalization of control over new bond issues in 1983, and the removal of restrictions governing the banks' lending rates of interest and the scrapping of credit ceilings in 1985), which had previously provided the SAP with an important, if limited, measure of influence in the capital market. The crisis period has also witnessed a dramatic development of new money market instruments. The state, for example, has recently issued a variety of securities (1980) and treasury bills (1982, 1983) in attempts both to meet its need for capital and to affect interest rates. However, unlike what occurred during the Social-Democratic Keynesian Era, the Swedish state and the Riksbank have been increasingly reduced to supplying attractive bonds to *persuade* the credit sector to purchase government securities (Kurzer, 1987). It should be clear that these developments have more to do with the global crisis and international trends than with which party (or bloc of parties) is at the helm, especially since some of the most central instances of deregulation occurred under SAP rule.

Other critical changes in the capital market became evident during this crisis period as well, but they were generated more out of the severe restrictions and regulations of the previous era than the economic crisis itself. For example, a large number of financial intermediaries, especially finance houses, emerged in the 1970s and 1980s, outside of the regulated credit market. Exempt from numerous credit controls, including lending ceilings, they grew in importance from 1975, when 79 finance houses provided 7 percent of all non-priority lending, to 1985, when 208 houses were responsible for 24 percent of the same (Kurzer, 1987). Moreover, almost half of them (45 percent) are actually subsidiaries created by the three large commercial banks to evade the restrictions of the Riksbank.

The banks were not alone in creating finance companies. Higher profits and the demands of some corporate managers for more autonomy have led a number of Sweden's major multinationals, such as ASEA, Alfa-Laval, and Volvo, to become somewhat less dependent on their "home" bank (Skandinaviska Enskilda Banken) by creating "internal" finance companies and capital groups, or by shopping globally for the best financial deals. The Volvo conglomerate, for example, has created a financial subsidiary called Volvofinans with liquid assets equivalent to those of Sweden's sixth largest bank (Hellier, 1985; Kapstein, 1988). As a result of the global crisis, the SAP was encouraged to deregulate rather than simply expand its system of controls to cover these new intermediary institutions. These developments, of course, further reduced the SAP's influence in the credit market.

If the potential of the three AP funds to influence the sectoral allocation of capital had been hampered from the start by legal restrictions, which allowed only indirect investments through banks or other specialized institutions, it became even more diminished during the late 1970s. While accounting for over 35 percent of all lending on the domestic credit market between 1970-1973, the funds' share had dropped to only 16 percent by 1979 as the numbers of pensioners drawing on them swelled and the average size of pensions increased (Martin, 1981; Pontusson, 1984a). Concerned both with increasing investment and with extending societal influence over investment to guide structural change, the LO called upon the SAP in the early 1970s to remove the restrictions preventing the three AP funds from owning equity capital. Instead, a fourth AP fund was created in 1974 which was authorized to purchase shares. However, because the SAP (with support from the Swedish Communist Party, VPK) and the bourgeois bloc held exactly the same number of seats in the Riksdag during this period, the latter bloc was able to ensure that the fourth fund played a very limited role in the capital market. Initially the fourth fund's growth was curtailed by restricting its purchases to no more than 10 percent of the equity in a single firm (1979), and preventing it from buying shares in enterprises which would have allowed more influence over the allocation of capital, such as insurance companies or banks.

During the Social-Democratic Keynesian Era, bank domination in the capital market was decreased to an admittedly limited but significant extent as a result of the power exercised by the SAP. In the Crisis Era, this process began to reverse as the state lost the capacity to exert influence in the financial market, and its instruments of control were being gradually phased out. Other developments, more in line with capital market-based financial systems, (such as the emergence of internal finance companies and the enormous growth of the Swedish stock market), have also meant a reduction in power for the SAP and, consequently, an increase in the power of capital.

Concentration, internationalisation and the rise of the export sector in the 1970s and 1980s

Concentration and internationalization in the Swedish economy are two closely interrelated processes, particularly since the latter half of the 1960s. The most concentrated industries in Sweden are the large multinational export industries, many of which expanded by creating subsidiaries and/or taking over competitors abroad. These developments both signalled and contributed to the ascendance of export capital and the decline of primarily home-market capital in the 1970s and 1980s. Once the engine of economic growth and development, home-market capital steadily and rapidly declined in importance in tandem with the economic crisis, except for a brief period in 1973-74 when it benefitted from the worldwide boom in raw materials. By 1983, only five of Sweden's fifteen top companies were engaged in the production of raw materials, whereas in 1925 the number was ten. Of course, many home-market manufacturers previously involved in the production of raw materials had transformed themselves into advanced, "high-tech" industries primarily oriented toward export markets and engaged in production abroad (Jagrén, 1986; Swedish Institute, 1986).

According to almost any measure, concentration has increased dramatically in Sweden during the last two decades, most notably among the export industries. One telling indicator is the concentration of employment. By 1976, approximately 76 percent of the total number of employees in the largest two hundred Swedish enterprises were concentrated in the fifty largest companies (Israel, 1978). By 1983, the ten largest corporations in Sweden accounted for 36.2 percent of employment in manufacturing (more than twice that found in Canada, Great Britain, France, Germany or Italy, over three times that found in the United States, and almost seven times that found in Japan), while the largest forty corporations" share of manufacturing employment was 57.0 percent (see Table 3.1).

The spate of mergers that erupted in the late 1960s persisted throughout the 1970s and 1980s. This was encouraged by tax laws that exempted companies with holdings of 25 percent or more in another firm from paying taxes on the dividends they received (Hellier, 1985). Between 1970 and 1976 alone, over 3,700 mergers took place (Israel, 1978). By the end of the decade, the number of mergers had increased to approximately 7,000 (Svensson, 1986). The most significant merger to take place during this period occurred in 1972, when two of Sweden's largest banks, the Enskilda Bank (the Wallenberg family bank) and the Skandinaviska Bank, both closely linked with the largest export corporations in Sweden through their respective holding companies, amalgamated. This resulted in the creation of the largest private bank in Scandinavia, the Skandinaviska Enskilda Bank (SEB) and solidified the Wallenberg empire's position as the most powerful force in Sweden. The linchpin of the Wallenberg sphere, the SEB holds sway over a federation of more than twenty very large, world-class, export-oriented Swedish industries, including Alfa-Laval, ASEA, Atlas Copco, Electrolux, L. M. Ericsson, Saab-Scania, SKF, and Swedish Match, through its three holding companies, Investor, Providentia and Export-Invest. Figure 3.1 provides only a partial listing of the companies comprising the Wallenberg empire in 1984.

Table 3.1
The Share of Employment in the Largest Corporations Compared to Total Manufacturing Employment, 1983

Country	Corporations			
	5 Largest	10 Largest	20 Largest	40 Largest
Canada	11.8	16.7	---	---
France	11.5	17.1	---	---
Germany	10.8	16.5	21.6	---
Great Britain*	10.6	16.8	25.5	---
Italy	13.6	15.3	---	---
Japan	3.4	5.2	7.2	---
Netherlands*	35.4	---	---	---
Sweden	21.6	36.2	46.4	57.0
Switzerland	53.7	73.2	---	---
USA**	7.9	11.2	15.3	21.4

* Shell and Unilever excluded.
** 1984.

Source: Jagrén (1986:41).

By the late 1970s, a number of the seventeen large ownership groups (Wehtje, Dunker, Broström and others) had declined in prominence and were taken over by or merged with larger conglomerates. The family ownership groups which had dominated in the previous era were increasingly replaced by "institutional" ownership in the 1970s and 1980s (i.e., indirect ownership through "legal persons" such as insurance companies, investment companies, foundations, and various types of funds which, in turn, are owned by one or more other groups). A recent government investigation of the structure of ownership and influence in the Swedish economy in the mid-1980s indicated that the level of concentration in Sweden had increased and highlighted the dominating position held by four main ownership groups: the Wallenberg empire, the closely linked Volvo and Skanska spheres (with control over a number of large export-oriented industries which include Euroc, Opus,

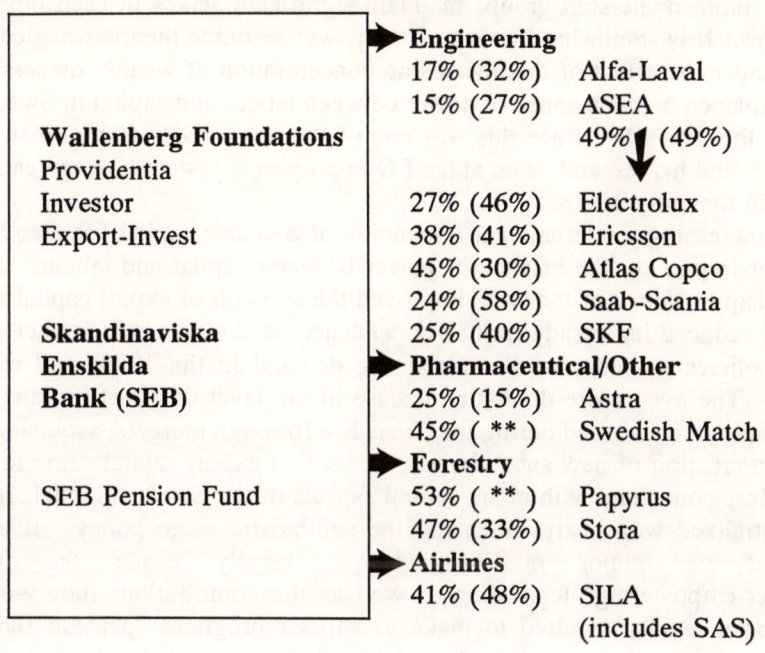

Note: The percentages in parantheses refer to 1990.

* Sila is controlled through a number of Wallenberg Companies.
** Stora has recently taken over both Papyrus and Swedish Match.

Source: Arbose and Skole (1984), Economist (June, 1990).

Figure 3.1 The Wallenberg Empire, 1984[9]

Pharmacia, Sandvik, Skanska, and Volvo), and the Industrivärden-Svenska Handelsbank group (AGA, L. M. Ericsson, SCA, Volvo) (Hermansson, 1987; Isaksson and Skog, 1987; The Economist, April, 1987). Other central, if less important, ownership groups include the Penser sphere (Bofors, Broström, Kema Nobel), the Lundberg sphere (Alfa-Laval, Siab, Östgöta Enskilda Bank), and the Ax:son Johnson, Bonnier, Lindholm, ABV-Pronator, Södeberg, Boliden, Kemp/Carlgren and Stenbeck spheres (Sundqvist, 1987). Most of the main ownership groups in Sweden are intimately connected, holding stock and directorships in each other's companies. Since the late 1970s, there has been a growing trend towards "cross ownership," whereby two or more ownership groups maintain significant stakes in each other's concerns. It is somewhat ironic that the power resource theorists neglected to consider the effect of this increasing concentration of wealth, ownership and influence on the balance of power between labour and capital in Sweden during the Crisis Era since this was one of the three major factors that led Meidner and his research team at the LO to propose a system of wage-earner funds in the early 1970s.

The increasingly international orientation of Swedish capital has also had a major impact on the balance of power between capital and labour. The rising export shares of the GDP improved the strength of export capital and greatly reduced its already limited dependence on the domestic market and state policies geared toward maintaining demand in the 1970s and early 1980s. The even more dramatic increase in the level of direct investment and employment abroad during the Crisis Era (through mergers, acquisitions and the creation of new subsidiaries), meant that export capital came to be much less concerned with many central aspects of the Swedish model, such as centralized wage bargaining and the solidaristic wage policy. It also allowed the major multinationals to largely evade the new "worker-empowering" legislation as well as the contributions they would have been legally required to make to various programs (pension funds, wage-earner funds, renewal funds and so on) if they carried out production domestically. In short, these new developments enabled export capital to begin undermining the historical compromise that capital, under the dominant leadership of the home-market faction, had reached with labour during the Social-Democratic Era.

The declining significance of the domestic market for Swedish corporations is easily demonstrated. As early as 1977, almost one-third of Sweden's GNP was being exported; between 1960 and 1975 the export share of Swedish industry rose from approximately 25 percent to 38 percent and increased at approximately the same rate during the following seven years; between 1965 and 1978 the Swedish multinationals' percentage of foreign sales jumped from 52 percent to 70 percent (including production abroad); between 1975 and 1982 the engineering industries' share of production for export had risen from 48 percent to 58 percent (Erixon, 1985, 1988; Hörnell and Vahlne, 1986; Sweden Now, 1977). By 1983, foreign sales accounted for 76 percent of the total sales of the largest twenty Swedish multinationals. However, more important than the increasing sales abroad were the escalating levels of direct investment beyond the Swedish borders. This is particularly true after 1960, when more than 75 percent of the manufacturing subsidiaries established abroad between 1975 and 1978 were founded (Skandinaviska Enskilda Banken, n.d.). After 1974, production outside Sweden increased twice as fast as exports did, decisively shifting the multinationals' gravitational centre abroad.

By the end of 1986, the eighty largest firms in Sweden accounted for approximately 370,000 employees abroad -- about twice as many as in 1965. The internationalization of the Swedish economy appears to be even more remarkable when the largest multinationals alone are examined. For example, in the 1980s the seventeen largest firms with foreign subsidiaries maintained over half of their total employment, between 35-45 percent of their investments, and almost 47 percent of their total assets abroad (Hermansson, 1987). Of the twenty largest Swedish multinationals in 1983, nineteen had foreign sales accounting for over half of their total sales, while the foreign sales of five of these companies was over 90 percent (see Table 3.2).

Although "market-oriented," the primary reasons that led the large Swedish export companies to engage in and accelerate production abroad did not involve the conventional search for cheaper sources of raw materials or labour. Rather, they sought to circumvent natural and artificial barriers to imported products, establish closer ties with buyers, gain access to large national markets, and take advantage of subsidies for domestic producers (SOU, 1983, no.17; Swedenberg, 1985). Thus, the bulk of the foreign direct investment has been highly concentrated in the industrialized countries, particularly in the EEC countries, rather than in the Third World. A large and growing proportion of this direct investment has involved the acquisition of existing companies abroad, rather than the establishment of new subsidiaries. While representing under 40 percent of foreign direct investment in the 1960s, acquisitions accounted for over 60 percent in the 1970s, as Swedish multinationals attempted to increase their market share, buy out a competitor, or become more vertically integrated (Hörnell and Vahlne, 1986). This trend has continued into the 1990s.

Portfolio investment abroad has been "all but ruled out" by Swedish foreign exchange laws, but regulations concerning foreign direct investment have obviously been applied very liberally (Swedenberg, 1979, 1985). To ensure a positive effect on the trade balance, the Riksbank has formally required Swedish firms wishing to invest abroad to first obtain permission from its Exchange Control Board, but such permission has virtually always been granted. For example, in 1977 only 13 of 1340 applications were refused (Hörnell and Vahlne, 1983). In 1960, permission was granted by the Board for direct investment abroad worth 288 million kronor. By 1978, permission was obtained for well over 3 billion kronor. These figures grossly underestimate the amount of direct investment abroad since they

Table 3.2
The 20 Largest Swedish Multinationals

Company Name	Employees abroad		Foreign sales as a percentage of total	Main products
	Number	Percentage of total		
AGA (1)*	7,662	68	69	Industrial gases
Alfa-Laval (2)	10,352	65	90	Farm/dairy equipment
ASEA (2)	11,582	27	65	Electrical equipment
Astra (2)	3,206	51	80	Pharmaceuticals
Atlas Copco (2)	11,996	71	91	Compressors
Electrolux (2)	58,372	66	76	Electrical appliances
Ericsson (1/2)	37,746	54	80	Telecommunications
ESAB (3/2)	4,123	71	91	Welding equipment
Esselte (4)	8,734	57	65	Office equipment
Euroc (5)	3,436	42	56	Construction equipment
Fläkt (3/2)	7,841	57	77	Environmental control
Incentive (6)	3,277	31	59	Heating

76

Table 3.2 (continued)

Saab-Scania (2)	6,939	18	Motor vehicles/planes
Sandvik (5)	14,807	58	Tools
Skanska (5)	8,502	31	Construction
SKF (5/2)	37,472	81	Rolling bearings
Sonesson	3,518	53	Power systems
SCA (1)	5,452	36	Pulp and paper
Swedish Match (2)	11,760	64	Flooring, matches, chemicals
Volvo (1/7)	15,541	22	Motor vehicles
	59		
	91		
	23		
	92		
	73		
	67		
	75		
	85		

Adapted from: Hörnell and Vahlne (1986), Sundqvist (1987).

* Numbers in parentheses indicate ownership sphere, 1986: 1 = SHB (Svenska Handelsbanken), 2 = Wallenberg, 3 = ASEA, 4 = Lindholm, 5 = Skanska, 6 = Lundberg, 7 = Volvo.

include neither the investments that Swedish companies finance abroad (which are not guaranteed by the Swedish parent) nor investments financed through the profits made by the subsidiaries abroad, both of which do not require permission from the Riksbank. Moreover, since 1981, in keeping with the deregulation taking place in the credit market, Swedish firms no longer have to demonstrate that their foreign investments will benefit the balance of payments to receive Riksbank authorization to invest abroad (Skandinaviska Enskilda Banken, n.d.). The strict regulations requiring Swedish multinationals to repatriate and reconvert (into devalued Swedish kronor) almost all of their export earnings has also resulted in higher levels of foreign investment. By expanding their foreign base, Swedish companies can more easily justify maintaining a larger share of their export earnings abroad to cover the costs of their operations (Kurzer, 1987). Whatever the validity of studies which have concluded that a high degree of concentration and higher levels of direct investment abroad are necessary for the long-term survival of Sweden's major multinationals, it is evident that these developments do not bode well for Swedish labour.

The wrangle over wage-earner funds: unity on the right

Throughout the 1970s, a wide variety of proposals for the creation of some type of "fund" were set out by the various political and economic organizations in Sweden as the international economic crisis unfolded, and acted upon the Swedish economy in diverse ways. The relative prosperity of the 1960s and the profit explosion in 1973-74 generated concern over the increasing concentration of power and wealth, the growing investment crisis which corresponded with the increasing internationalization of Swedish capital, and wage drift and the consequent undermining of the solidaristic wage policy. The latter half of the 1970s witnessed severely declining levels of profitability. This was a result of the 1975-76 wage explosion (triggered by the profits explosion), the after-effects of the oil shocks, and the "cost crisis" generated by higher payroll taxes and the appreciation of the Swedish krona due to Sweden's cooperation with the European Currency Snake. During this period, new concerns were raised regarding inadequate savings and investment quotas, the lack of risk capital, the security of the pension system, and increasing speculation. The various concerns were reflected in the disparate fund proposals developed in the 1970s by organizations on the Right as well as the Left. However, by the early 1980s, largely in response to the concerted efforts of the SAF (and the nature of labour's demands), a degree of cohesion reminiscent of the 1940s was achieved by the business community, the various employer associations, and the bourgeois parties in their opposition to any form of wage-earner funds.

In 1974, during the period of the "lottery government" - so called because the equal number of seats held by the socialist and non-socialist blocs in the Riksdag meant that lots had to be drawn to break ties - the SAP, without consulting the LO leadership, assented to a suggestion made by the Liberal Party during the Haga discussions calling for the establishment of a Royal Commission to investigate the issue of employee participation in the growth of company capital. Established in 1975, the Royal Commission, composed of representatives of the central employer organizations (SAF, SI, SHIO-Familjeföretagen), the main employee federations (LO, TCO, SACO/SR), and the four major political parties (Conservative, Liberal, Centre, SAP), and chaired by a succession of Social Democrats (Hjalmar Mehr 1975-79, Allan Larsson 1979-81, Berndt Öhman 1981), had produced countless reports and a wealth of factual information by the time it disassembled in 1981. However, in striking contrast with earlier joint investigations, this Commission had thoroughly failed to produce a fund proposal around which even a modest degree of consensus could be reached. For the most part, the members of the committee refused to stray very far from the fund proposal or position set out by the economic or political group they represented.

Concerned with concentration in the Swedish economy and the need for increased capital formation, the Liberal Party (Folkpartiet) presented a memorandum on wage-earner funds in 1978. The memorandum called for a compulsory system of general (rather than company-based) funds to be financed by contributions based on wages and, possibly, on the "excess profits" of larger companies -- although the latter would not take the form of compulsory share issues as suggested by Meidner. However, the most contentious aspect of this proposal was its insistence on individual shareholdings, rather than the collectively-owned shares the LO demanded. Like the Liberal Party, the Centre Party resolved that the fund shares be held individually, although it did not formulate a proposal of its own (Öhman, 1984). Strongly critical of the Meidner Plan and the later LO/SAP proposals, the Conservative Party -- since 1969 styled as the Moderate Party (Moderata Samlingspartiet) -- rejected the idea of wage-earner funds altogether and recommended incentives for voluntary saving, which were, in fact, introduced in 1978 while the bourgeois parties were in office. Also opposed to any proposal advocating collective shares, the powerful employers' association, SI, under the direction of Erland Waldenström, had presented a report in 1976 (the *Waldenström Report*) which called for *voluntary* profit-sharing on the company level (Rehn, 1983; Richardson,

1982). Amidst this ideological cacophony of resolute proposals, the SAF was able to assume the role of power broker.

Of the more than nine hundred different employer organizations in Sweden, the SAF is by far the most important and powerful. Acting on behalf of over 38,000 private sector manufacturing, construction, commerce, transport and service companies that employ over 3.1 million people and are affiliated with its 37 sectoral associations, SAF has not ordinarily operated as an overtly political organization. Rather, it has functioned as the principal negotiating body for employers and sought to insure its members against financial losses in the event of labour disputes (Leion, 1985; Hammarström, 1987; Skogh, 1984). However, this changed in the latter half of the 1970s as the SAF came to be dominated by export capital. This "changing of the guard" was realized in SAF's new leadership. In 1976, Curt Nicolin, one of the top executives in the Wallenberg empire and chairman of ASEA, replaced Tryggve Holm as Chairman of the Board and, two years later, Olof Ljunggren assumed the role of Managing Director, previously held by Curt-Steffan Giesecke. Together these two arch-conservatives, rejecting the Swedish model and the compromise on which it was based, set out to reorganize and reorient the SAF and prepared for a lengthy and bitter battle with labour (De Geer, 1987; Larsson, 1987).

In the early 1970s, in the face of increasing labour radicalism, the leadership of the two largest and most powerful employer associations, SI and SAF, were willing to continue to cooperate with the SAP, but the members of these organizations were beginning to rebel. This was reflected in their refusal to support the SI-sponsored *Waldenström Report* on wage-earner funds, which they regarded as too conciliatory (De Geer, 1987). The numerous, mostly small-scale industries in Sweden organized under the SHIO-Familjeföretagen (Swedish Federation of Crafts and Small and Medium-Sized Companies -- Swedish Association of Family Enterprises) were particulary opposed to any further encroachment on their control in the workplace, and labour's proposals for wage-earner funds. With new leaders at the helm in the late 1970s, the SAF determined to take advantage of this burgeoning discontent and reverse the drift to the left, which had taken place over the previous decade. While this would not happen "overnight," the wage-earner fund issue provided the perfect vehicle with which to mobilise the employers and mount an ideological attack and unify capital, large and small, home-market and export.

The SAF's "counter-offensive" included the use of tactics normally associated with labour. For example, in 1977 the SAF held its first-ever Congress. Because such a body was not provided for in the SAF statutes, the Congress was, unlike its union counterpart, only advisory. Nevertheless, this and later Congresses provided a forum in which capitalists could reaffirm their faith in the market economy, and legitimized the SAF as a popular movement. In addition to diatribes concerning the creation of "trade union funds," numerous reports critical of the growing public sector, the high marginal taxation rate, the solidaristic wage policy, and the job-security legislation, which had just been passed, were also presented at the SAF Congresses (Faxén, 1977; Johnston, 1977; Ståhl, 1977; Westholm, 1977).

Another strategy which SAF borrowed from the labour movement and used to great advantage was the mass demonstration. Gunnar Randholm, managing director of an industrial conglomerate (Eldon) and a member of the SAF's Board of Directors, headed a committee of twenty-four businessmen that orchestrated the highly-publicized and highly-successful "Fourth of October" demonstration in which 75,000 to 100,000 small and large company owners, representatives of business and industry, and other opponents of "fund socialism" from around the country marched through Stockholm to the parliament building where SAP was introducing its wage-earner fund bill. Although the numbers have dwindled considerably since the first demonstration in 1983, the business community has continued to "celebrate" and hold demonstrations on the fourth of October to register its opposition to the funds and remind the public of the SAP's "commitment to socialism."

In an address given at a meeting of the IOE (International Organization of Employers) Executive Committee in 1980, the SAF's Managing Director, Olof Ljunggren, acknowledged the increasingly political role played by the SAF and emphasized the need for it to continue to "step up [its] activities in the field of information and the formation of public opinion":

> Of course, we have always taken social policy aspects into account in our work. But there is a vast difference between the nature of our involvement today and that of, say 10 years ago. Nowadays we seek to give publicity to our standpoint in order to achieve effects on public opinion that will influence the government, the public, and the bureaucrats (Ljunggren, 1980:7).

In Sweden, where businesses and employer associations are not allowed to make direct contributions to political parties, influencing public opinion is of paramount importance. To this end, the SAF engaged in an anti-fund media blitz which even surpassed their PHM campaign of the 1940s. It sponsored a series of seminars and public discussions, advertised on billboards, mailed out flyers and provided press releases, plastered posters on the walls of subways and bus stops, provided educational materials to the schools, and encouraged employers and managers to speak out against the funds on the radio, on television and in the newspapers. It also trained some 20,000 employers to inform their employees of the nature of the proposed funds. Fearing a return of the SAP and its wage-earner fund program in 1983, the SAF undertook special measures in 1982 to persuade people working with the public (taxi drivers, hairdressers, gas station attendants, and so on) to spread its anti-fund message (Hansson, 1984). Per Olof-Edin, head of LO's research department and architect of the 1983 fund program, recently admitted that the LO could not begin to meet the challenge of this barrage of propaganda and estimated that the resources utilized by the SAF (money and people) were ten times greater than that which the LO was able to muster (Edin, 1987). According to another source, Swedish business organizations spent 55-60 million kronor during the 1982 election campaign on their wage-earner fund propaganda alone -- almost as much as the combined total spent by Sweden's five largest political parties on their entire election campaigns for that year (Hansson, 1984).

In 1980, the SAF placed another neo-Liberal member of the "new guard" in a key position -- editor-in-chief of SAF's weekly newspaper -- who immediately changed the paper's name (from Arbetsgivaren to SAF-tidningen) as well as its ideological perspective, publishing articles which were not only critical of the various proposals for wage-earner funds but also of the "historical compromise" and the Swedish model itself. Similar views were put forward in publications originating from SAF-controlled organizations such as Näringslivets Ekonomifakta, Industriförbundet and IUI (The Industrial Institute for Economic and Social Research) (Broström, 1986). In addition, the SAF created a number of new publishing companies, such as Timbro and Ratio, to promote its own pro-market publications and provide translations of books by Friedrich Hayek and numerous other liberals. These publications were sold to the public through one of the SAF's outlets and distributed to the large conservative and liberal newspaper chains, which dominate in Sweden, ensuring that SAF's message found its way into the editorial pages (Gustafsson, 1987).

With a combined circulation of over three million and accounting for over 68 percent of the daily press (Sweden Now, 1973), the liberal and conservative newspapers supporting the three bourgeois parties published countless articles attacking the LO/SAP proposals for wage-earner funds, often conjuring up images of Eastern-European Communism. A representative article, but probably one of the most influential because it was written by Assar Lindbeck, a leading Swedish economist and SAP member. Lindbeck's departure from the party because of its commitment to wage-earner funds was much publicized. His article was published in the liberal daily, Dagens Nyheter, shortly after the LO Congress in 1976:

What is stated by the proposers to be continuous proceeding of traditional Swedish reform activity is in fact just as destructive for the economic system as the socializations arising in Eastern Europe after the second world war, however with the difference that a "private" organization, the trade union movement, should take the place of the Government as the owner and employers organization -- at the same time as the same organization claims to represent the employees ... I believe that not many of us would like to live in the society that would be the probable result of Meidner's trade union funds. There is, in my opinion, no more important task in Swedish political debate today than to warn the Swedish people of Meidner's and the LO-Congress proposal (Lindbeck, 1976:3).

The efforts of the SAF proved successful. Poll after poll indicated a growing opposition to the idea of collective wage-earner funds. By 1982, 57 percent of the public opposed them, 27 percent were undecided and only 15 percent of the public were in favour of them (Lyon, 1985).[10] Having united the employers' associations and the business community, and having significantly influenced public opinion, the SAF would not have to work as hard to unite the bourgeois parties. Between 1976 and 1982 the Conservative Party, riding with an international wave of market populism, captured an increasingly larger share of the popular vote at the expense of the Liberal and the Centre parties. Nevertheless, the SAF found it expedient to meet with members of the Liberal and Centre parties who were disposed toward reaching a compromise with the LO and the SAP on the question of wage-earner funds in order to persuade them to change their views (Schager, 1987). By 1982, a solid bloc of opposition had been created on the Right when the Liberal Party, and the Centre Party allied with the Conservative Party and the employers associations. (A summary of the organization and unity of capital in each of the three eras discussed above is presented in Table 3.3.)

Conclusion

During the Crisis Era, changes in the organization and unity of capital, which had begun much earlier, significantly altered the balance of power between labour and capital in favour of the latter. Rapidly advancing levels of concentration in the late 1950s and 1960s escalated even more quickly in the 1970s and 1980s. At the same time, the Swedish economy became increasingly export-oriented, both in terms of sales and, more importantly, production abroad. As a result of these trends, capital became less factionalized along home-market/export lines. The unification of capital was helped along by the international crisis, which served to eliminate some home-market industries engaged in the production of raw materials. The creation of a much larger and more unified bloc of (export) capital, which was increasingly independent of the domestic economy, capital's re-orientation and the politicization of key business associations, and the deregulation in the financial market brought on by the economic crisis in the 1970s and 1980s clearly increased the power of capital vis-à-vis that of labour. Not only was the wage-earner fund program diluted, leaving it a mere shadow of the original proposal. Capital also attacked the historical compromise it had previously supported under the dominance of home-market capital, now rejecting centralized bargaining, the solidaristic wage policy and the welfare state. And it sought to cut taxes, further deregulate, and restore market forces. Power resource theorists have tended to ignore such tendencies as well as the way in which the SAP's reformist policies have contributed to their development. It should not be concluded, however, that labour would have been able to push through its wage-earner fund plan if capital had not increased its power as documented above. Labour was far too divided on the fund issue.

Table 3.3
Organization and Unity of Capital in Sweden

Measures of the Organization and Unity of Capital	Liberal Era (1820-1932)	Social-Democratic Keynesian Era (1932-76)	Crisis Era (1976-84)*
Dominant faction of Capital/ Growth Strategy	Home-Market sector	Home-Market sector	Export sector
Type of Financial System	Bank-dominated	Bank-dominated with considerable state influence	Bank-dominated with declining state influence
Concentration of Capital	Relatively low levels	Wave of mergers in '60s and '70s	Continued escalation
Internationalisation	Relatively low levels	Beginning to escalate in '50s, '60s, '70s	Continued escalation
Control over/ Orientation of Business Associations	Creation of SAF (1902)/ Functional	Controlled by home-market sector/ Functional	Controlled by export sector/ Overtly political

* The changes in the organization and unity of capital that took place during the Crisis Era have, of course, continued in the same direction since 1984, the year the wage-earner fund plan was introduced.

85

Notes

1. A number of authors have pointed to the failure of proponents of power resource theory to balance their accounts of labour's growing power resources by examining those of capital. "The problem is," as Hannu Uusitalo (1979:297) pointed out, "that increases of the power resources of the working class and the bourgeoisie are not matched together, and consequently the assumption of the gradual decrease of power difference is not supported by evidence." Jonas Pontusson (1984:82) makes the same point: "Conceived in organizational terms, 'strength of labour' is by no means coterminous with 'weakness of capital'." However, neither author goes on to examine the power of capital. Himmelstrand, et al. (1981) do address the issue of capital's strength, however summarily, but their conclusion that the strength of capital has declined over the past two decades is not supported by the findings of the present study.
2. Of course it is not only international developments that can lead to the development of new accumulation strategies. "Domestic" instability may also contribute to such a development. The increasing radicalization of the labour movement may, for example, encourage capital to increase levels of production abroad.
3. According to Laxer (1981:283) it was "the increasingly skewed distribution of incomes towards those at the top, despite the political strength of the farmers and later the Social Democrats [which] undoubtedly facilitated a higher saving rate and dampened consumption."
4. Although this was the "Liberal Era," the use of protectionist measures was quite common during periods of stress. They are "the orthodox deviation from free-market orthodoxy" (Gourevitch, 1986:44).
5. There is some disagreement concerning the periodization of dominance of the home-market and export factions of capital. Following Apple, Higgins and Wright (1981), Erixon (1987, 1988, 1989), and Kurzer (1987), the position taken here is that home-market capital was dominant during the Social-Democratic Era, although the increasing importance of export capital during the 1950s and 1960s is emphasised. Erixon (1988:6), for example, argues that "the postwar Keynesian accord was e.g. based on a strong home-market oriented faction within Swedish industry including firms within construction and food, textiles, engineering and iron- and steel industries." He further notes that the SAF's "co-operative and pragmatic attitude" toward labour and the SAP "reflected the strength of home-market industries." Part of the disagreement stems from the way "home-market capital" is

conceptualized. For some, the home-market faction of capital refers to "small business" and "suppliers." This is not the line followed here. Rather, "home-market capital" refers here to some of the large (and medium-sized) industries which were *primarily* engaged in the production of raw materials (originally) and highly dependent upon the domestic market for their labour force and their resources. They were also reliant upon the domestic market for a large part of their sales, if not a majority of them. An example of a home-market industry which was involved in engineering rather than in the production of raw materials during the Social-Democratic Keynesian Era would be the Volvo Corporation. Its exports amounted to little more than 1,000 vehicles per year as late as the 1950s and it has only relatively recently emerged as an exporter of passenger cars. By the 1980s, approximately 50 percent of Volvo's passenger cars were assembled abroad (Enström and Levinson, 1982) and the Swedish auto industry was exporting 75 percent of the automobiles it manufactured. L. M. Ericsson is a good example of an export industry which, before the turn of the century, had already set up its first foreign plant and was selling almost all of its products abroad. Another example is SKF which, by 1933, "was selling in 56 countries outside Sweden, had sales companies in 26 countries and manufacturing facilities in five countries" and 60 percent of its employees were foreigners (Hörnell and Vahlne, 1986:6). During the latter part of this Era, however, the dividing line became increasingly blurred as some home-market industries became more involved in engineering and both factions of capital increased their level of sales and production abroad.

By the 1970s the home-market and export factions of capital had become almost as one. However, the split between these factions during the Social-Democratic Keynesian Era should not be overlooked. In a letter to John Maynard Keynes, Marcus Wallenberg, a key representative of export capital -- particularly after the crash of the Ivar Kreuger Empire in 1932 and the redistribution of the Kreuger holdings in Swedish Match, L. M. Ericsson, SKF, SCA, Boliden, Stora Kopparberg, Grängesberg, Skandinaviska Banken and Svenska Handelsbanken, among others (Glete, 1978) -- maintained that public spending in Sweden represented "public extravagance" and a "violation of economic laws" (quoted in Clegg, Boreham, and Dow, 1986:379). And the representatives of export-capital had formed a group (the Directors' Club) in the 1930s in an attempt to block the SAP's Keynesian proposals and weaken the position of the unions. However, such attempts were thwarted by home-market capital (reflected in the Basic

Agreement reached between capital and labour) which, because of its dependence upon the domestic market, preferred to co-operate with SAP. As pointed out earlier, export capital was not interested in Keynesian or welfare policies designed to boost internal demand since it was not primarily reliant upon the domestic market. However, after its defeat, export capital became more accommodating and was taken into the compromise between home-market capital and labour as Gourevitch (1986) notes. As a result, many of the policies carried out by the SAP served the interests of "big capital," both home-market and export. This included not only the Rehn-Meidner model, which systematically eliminated the smaller and less-profitable companies, but the Investment Reserve Fund System and the 1938 tax reform as well. The latter involved "a series of corporate tax expenditures designed to lessen the tax burden on Sweden's biggest and most profitable corporations" (Steinmo, 1988:420).

6. Created in 1938, the investment reserve fund system (IF system) did not play an important role in the Swedish economy until 1955, when it was revised. The purpose of the IF system was to shift investment from boom to slack periods. It encouraged firms to set aside up to 40 percent of their profits -- 46 percent of which had to be deposited in interest-free accounts at the Riksbank. Then, if the firms withdrew a portion of the funds for domestic investment at a time specified by the government, they did not have to pay taxes on the amounts involved. While this system allowed the SAP to exert some influence over the timing of investment, it did not provide a means by which to influence the allocation of investment (Bergström, 1978; Bergström and Södersten, 1984).

7. In West Germany, according to Peter Hall (1984:25), the instruments of monetary policy are controlled by the Deutsche Bundesbank which is "relatively insulated" from pressure from the Ministry of Economics and parliament. The independence of the Bundesbank is guaranteed by the German constitution which gave it a mandate to protect the value of the currency and made it responsible for monetary and credit policy.

8. Of course this didn't prevent Swedish corporations from creating branch plants abroad. It only ensured that the majority of such investments were financed by long-term foreign currency borrowing. In the 1960s, "liberal treatment was given to applications to borrow abroad to finance outward direct investment and commercial credits" (OECD, 1982:28).

9. It should be noted that the Wallenberg group has even more control than this account of its approximate voting shares in various companies suggests. This is because of the existence of shares with different

voting strengths, referred to as Series A and Series B shares. Since the passage of the Swedish Companies Act in 1944, the voting strength of a Series A share cannot exceed ten times that of a Series B share. However, a "grandfather clause" allows companies which were issuing shares before the 1944 Act to maintain a much larger voting discrepancy between A and B shares. The Wallenberg group thus holds Series A shares in companies such as Alfa-Laval, Electrolux, Ericsson, and SKF which have 1,000 votes each (Hufford, 1977; Isaksson and Skog, 1987; Skole, 1987). The SEB is no longer as central to the Wallenberg Empire as it once was, although it retains its symbolic importance. The Wallenberg family only control about 8 percent of SEB now and most of the shares which the SEB once held in other companies have been transferred to the three investment companies.

10. A number of Swedish social democrats suggest that part of the reason that these polls indicate public disfavour for wage-earner funds is related to the way in which the questions were phrased. If the public was asked "do you prefer industrial policy-making to be concentrated in the hands of a few capitalists or shared by citizen employees through wage earner funds?", rather than, "If employees were given a large part of ownership in companies, should this in your opinion be done by giving stock to individual employees or by giving stock or shares to trade unions?", the response, they maintain, would be quite different (quoted in Lyon, 1986:580).

4 The ideological development of the SAP and disunity within the Swedish working class

Both the failures and successes of Swedish social democracy have been explained by the power resource model in terms of a single, structural determinant -- the level of power resources attained by the working class at a given historical conjuncture. The model's inability to adequately account for the deradicalization of the wage-earner fund program is partly due to its failure to examine concurrent developments in capital's power. In addition to this external obstacle, there are other factors, also ignored by power resource theory, that are *internal* to the Swedish labour movement and help to explain the latter's inability to bring about economic democracy in Sweden through its proposal for wage-earner funds.

The first internal factor to be examined is the SAP's commitment to socialism or economic democracy. Power resource theory assumes that the working class will automatically be disposed toward socialist goals once it has achieved a certain level of power and thus ignores the important role party ideologies and party leadership play in mobilizing and providing direction for the working class. In countries such as the United States and

Canada, for example, it is unlikely that even a very dramatic increase in the power resources of the working class would, alone, lead to socialism. Much depends on how such resources are marshalled by party leaders, guided by the commitments expressed in the ideology of the party.

A second important issue concerns the degree of unity between and within the SAP and the other branch of the labour movement, the LO, especially with regard to questions concerning economic democracy and wage-earner funds. Unity around these issues within the TCO, the other major labour federation (although it is not formally defined as part of the "labour movement"), and between it and the LO, is also of central importance. Quantitative measures of working class strength utilized by power resource theory, such as the percentage of the labour force that is unionised, can give a false impression of unity among the working class and mask fundamental rifts. It will be argued here that such internal divisions played an important role in the dilution of the original wage earner fund program.

Party ideology and disunity in the Swedish "labour movement"

The two classic accounts of SAP ideology which focus on the party's commitment to socialism are those of Herbert Tingsten, a former editor of a large liberal daily newspaper, and Leif Lewin, a prominent professor of political science at the University of Uppsala and a member of the SAP. Writing in the 1930s, Tingsten (1973) argued that the SAP had, by then, almost totally abandoned its Marxist heritage, and consequently its socialist program, and become a social reformist party. According to Tingsten, there were three reasons for the gradual departure from Marxism and socialism. First, Marxist theory was internally inconsistent. At one moment it called for social reform (the "minor perspective") while at the next it maintained such reform would contradict the laws of historical development and retard the development of socialism (the "major perspective"), thus preventing the possibility of voluntary action. Second, Marx's predictions regarding the impoverishment of the working class, the disappearance of the middle class, the tendency toward concentration in industry and agriculture and so on, had failed to materialize, as Bernstein had noted earlier. And third, the theory was inappropriate for a country such as Sweden where the economy was still largely agrarian-based. In one of the earliest articulations of the concept of the "end of ideology," Tingsten furthered maintained that since the Folkpartiet (Liberal Party) and the other major political parties had moved from classical liberalism toward social liberalism, politics in Sweden had become "depoliticized."

Critics of Tingsten's interpretation focus on his "superficial" and "deterministic" understanding of Marx (Korpi, 1978b; Stephens, 1981b), his subjective appraisal of what is deemed illogical and contradictory in Marxist theory (Sainsbury, 1981), his inability to account for the party's persistent interest in industrial and economic democracy (Sainsbury, 1981), and his over-emphasis on the importance of Marx's writings to Swedish social democracy and his consequent neglect of more central influences (Abrahamsson and Broström, 1980). While Tingsten did tend to place too much emphasis on Marx's influence at the expense of others', the SAP very much appreciated some of Marx's theoretical insights. This was made clear by Ernst Wigforss, a central figure and key party strategist within the SAP:

> We saw the whole economic development as an example of the correctness of the Marxian description of capitalist development. This was a precondition for our political strategy....we had to try to hasten the development towards big enterprises and thereby the need for economic planning which we had assumed in our program....The idea was thus to urge on the Marxian concentration, to the hasten the development which from the beginning we had seen as a condition for socialism (quoted in Korpi, 1983:49).

Tingsten's chief critic was Leif Lewin, whose study of the planned economy debate of the 1940s was aimed at Tingsten's account. Like Tingsten, Lewin (1975) also held that the SAP had abandoned some deterministic, Marxist dogmas, but he did not equate this with an abandonment of socialism. Rather, the SAP had simply become strategically reoriented while remaining committed to the goal of socialism. Moreover, the liberal notion of "freedom *from* the state" shared by the parties on the Right was very different from the social democratic belief in "freedom *for* the state."

While both these readings of the SAP's commitment to socialism provide valuable insights, neither allows for developments that occurred after they were written.[1] The SAP's planning offensive in the 1940s, for example, does not entirely fit with Tingsten's assertion that the party had almost completely forsaken its interest in socialism. On the other hand, the SAP's refusal to endorse the plan for wage-earner funds until it had been thoroughly "emasculated" provides little support for Lewin's notion that the party was still very committed to socialism. It will be argued here that the SAP ideology, as reflected in party programs, statements and policies, and in the speeches and writings of successive generations of its leading theoreticians, party leaders, and key ministers, has evolved through three broad stages with regard to its commitment to socialism. In each of these stages the party's understanding of the essential elements of a socialist society and how to achieve it was gradually redefined.[2] It should be emphasized that the primary concern here is with tracing the evolution of the SAP's ideological commitment to socialism and economic democracy (and highlighting the consequent divergence between the SAP and the LO) rather than with providing an explanation for that development.

During the first stage, from the party's origin in 1889 until it came to power in 1932, the SAP was formally committed to bringing about socialism. The nationalization of most, if not all, of Sweden's large industries, financial enterprises, and farms came to be viewed as the most direct and efficient means of doing so. During the second stage, the 1930s to 1960s, contrary to the interpretation provided by Tingsten, the SAP still expressed a strong interest in socialism but the emphasis was now on economic planning rather than on nationalization, which came to be seen as only one of many means of creating a socialist society. In the 1960s, the SAP entered a third stage, unanticipated by Lewin, in which it expressed a commitment to "functional socialism" only, a notion that grew out of the ideas of the previous stage. Thus, by the 1970s, the SAP was out of step with an increasingly radical LO and the latter's proposal for wage-earner funds, which had been developed and approved without the knowledge of the party -- the traditional characterisation of the LO and the SAP as "two branches of the same tree" notwithstanding.

It is important to remember that during none of the three stages set out here was there ever unanimity regarding the fundamental goals and ideals of the party and how to achieve them. As a result, many of the SAP's programmatic statements are purposely vague and open to interpretation so as to appeal to both the leftist and rightist factions within the party. Each of the three stages is characterized here according to the *dominant* view regarding the realization of socialism. Neither should these three stages be seen as discrete periods. Rather, each evolved from the theories and ideas of the previous stage. Of course, the actual policies carried out by the party during any of the stages may reflect more immediate and pragmatic concerns rather than the formally-stated commitment to socialism.

Evolutionary socialism and nationalisation: 1889-1932

Despite the growing interest in socialist ideas in Sweden by the middle of the nineteenth century -- evidenced, for example, by the translation of the *Communist Manifesto* into Swedish in 1848 -- socialist ideas had not yet established roots in the form of organizations or programs. As a result, the trade unions, which gradually began to emerge from the journeymen's societies after the abolition of the guild system in the mid-1800s, first came under the influence of the Liberals (Landauer, 1959a). The Swedish social democratic movement did not really begin to take shape until the latter part of the nineteenth century, with Sweden's comparatively late but rapid industrialization and the emergence of a burgeoning industrial proletariat. Therefore, it was profoundly influenced by its German counterpart and thus came to embrace gradualism and state socialism.

German ideas about socialism were imported into Sweden in the early 1880s by August Palm. While apprenticing as a tailor in Germany and Denmark, Palm was greatly influenced by the debates and discussions taking place abroad and soon returned to Sweden to propagandize and agitate for socialism. In 1882 the Swedish Social Democratic Workers' Association, founded by Palm, published in its journal, *Folkviljan* (The People's Will), the first Swedish social democratic program. Significantly, it was essentially a carbon copy of the Danish Social Democrats' 1876 Gimle Program which was itself derived from the German Gotha Program (Tingsten, 1973). Endorsed by the German Social Democratic Party (SPD) in 1875, the Gotha Program was guided by a theory of the state which was much more dependent upon the ideas of Ferdinand Lassalle than upon Marxism. The Lassallean view of the state as an association of the population that could be used to legislate a socialist order gradually and the Lassallean commitment to state socialism were adopted holus bolus by the nascent Swedish social democratic movement.

By the end of the decade, in 1889, over 70 workers' organizations -- craft and industrial unions, political clubs and so on -- combined to create the Swedish Social Democratic Party, SAP. Predictably, its first party program, drafted by Axel Danielsson and adopted in 1897, was based on the program the SPD had endorsed at its 1891 Congress in Erfurt. However, while the Erfurt Program marked the SPD's return to Marxist doctrine via Kautsky, it was evident that the SAP had been influenced both by the Bernsteinian critique of Marxism and by Fabian currents from England (which had developed in the years preceding the program's adoption), and that the Swedish social democrats, in the main, continued to accept Lassalle's positive view of the capitalist state. While affirming the SAP's commitment to a socialist transformation, the program made it clear that such a transition would be evolutionary and not revolutionary -- despite the existence of a small radical, Marxist faction within the party:

> Social Democracy differs from other political parties in that it aspires to completely transform the economic organization of bourgeois society and bring about the social liberation of the

working class to secure and develop intellectual and material culture...

This, in turn, can only come about through the abolition of the monopoly of private capital on the means of production and their transformation into the common property of all society, together with the replacement of the planless production of commodities by a socialist production that meets the real needs of society.

Social Democracy therefore wishes to bring about the political organization of the working class as well, to take possession of public power, and *gradually* convert the means of production -- transportation, forests, mines, mills, machines, factories, the land -- into community property (quoted in Tingsten, 1973:118-119, emphasis added).

If the SAP was programmatically committed to socialism, in practice "the Party may be said to have followed the revisionist line from the start..." (Severin, 1956a:217). Under the leadership of Hjalmar Branting, a former member of the Liberal movement who became, by far, the most central figure in Swedish social democracy during this stage, the SAP pursued a "Swedish variant of revisionism," which was clearly dependent upon Bernstein, despite its "Marxist colouring" (Abrahamsson and Broström, 1980). This entailed cooperation with the Liberal Party in the struggle to achieve universal suffrage. Such cooperation included the participation of Branting and three other social democrats in the Liberal cabinet of 1917, and the modest reforms proposed by the SAP minority governments of 1920, 1921-23 and 1924-26.[3] Certain officials within the SAP such as F.V. Thorsson, the party's financial expert, and Bernhard Eriksson, a chief spokesperson on social policy, expressed strong reservations about nationalization. The latter, for example, stated that

there is much truth in our opponent's observation that state management is not as economically advantageous as private management. This above all because of the bureaucratization inside state apparatuses. On the whole it is doubtful whether the state is suited to administer economic firms (quoted in Tilton, 1987:144).

Other members of the SAP executive such as Gustav Möller, the party secretary and future Minister of Social Affairs, and Branting himself did not share such reservations. However, they stressed "socialization" rather than "nationalization."[4]

Declining party membership and electoral support, the SAP's minority status, and the post-war recession may have prevented it from pursuing more radical policies while in power, but the SAP was still ideologically committed to socializing the Swedish economy. However, from the turn of the century, the SAP gradually begun to rethink its strategy for doing so. In a country which was still largely, if no longer primarily, agricultural, the SAP had sought to assist and protect the small landholder from the encroachment of powerful industrial developers through changes to its 1905 and 1911 party programs. This was done for reasons both of tactics and principle. By 1920, the party program explicitly referred to selective nationalization: "*All* natural resources, industrial enterprises, financial institutions, means of transportation and communication *necessary to introduce a planned economy* are to be transferred to public ownership" (quoted in Sainsbury, 1980:26). It also introduced the idea of worker and consumer participation in the administration of state undertakings, and in the same year the SAP created a Commission on industrial democracy as well as one on socialization. For the first time, the SAP now emphasized planning as the central task of socialism, and party discussions at the 1920 Congress indicated the party now believed that to preserve a certain level of competition and prevent the stagnation which would likely accompany state monopoly, it should neither suppress new private initiative nor nationalize all existing private enterprises (Landauer, 1959b; Severin, 1956b). Despite the calls the SAP's 1928 program made for the nationalization of natural resources, it can be said that throughout the 1920s, the SAP gradually abandoned its commitment to large-scale nationalisation as its primary objective upon attaining power.[5]

The relationship between the SAP and the LO was, of course, very close during the first stage set out here. Indeed, the SAP, which placed great priority on and played the central role in organizing unions, had established the LO as a separate, central body in 1898 to take over the party's economic functions, such as providing support for unions during situations of conflict. At first the various union branches were required to become collective members of the SAP. However, to attract some of the larger unions, compulsory collective affiliation and the party's right to appoint members to the LO executive board were rescinded two years later. By 1908, individual union members were allowed to submit "reservations" against collective affiliation by their union, thereby permitting their exemption from party membership. The following year, the Branting resolution, consisting of obligations tying the unions to party programs, was also abolished (Blake, 1960; Carlson, 1969; Elvander, 1974).

Despite the severing of these formal links, the two bodies remained closely tied to, and dependent upon, one another. The first LO chair, Frederik Sterky, was a key social democrat and the editor of an SAP journal, while his successor, Herman Lindqvist, who held the position for twenty years, also became a member in Branting's cabinet. During this period the organizational, financial and electoral links between the LO and the SAP were firmly established, strengthening the labour movement. However, this period also witnessed the creation of opposition from the left of the SAP when a group of anarchists, syndicalists and socialists broke away from the SAP in 1917 to form the Social Democratic Left Party, -- the political ancestor of the present Left Communist Party (VPK, Vänsterpartiet Kommunisterna).

Economic planning, social reform and the "people's home": 1932-1960s

In the 1930s and 1940s, the SAP became increasingly absorbed in its planned economy approach as an independent means of creating socialism, and began to question whether even the piecemeal nationalization that had been proposed earlier was very useful. Nationalization came to be viewed not so much as a means of creating socialism as an instrument that could occasionally be utilized to improve the economy's performance (Lewin, 1975; Sainsbury, 1980). During this stage, many of the ideas introduced in the 1920s were further elaborated upon by the central members of a "second generation" of social democrats such as Per Albin Hansson (the People's Home), Nils Karleby (the notion of property as a "bundle of rights"), Ernst Wigforss (industrial democracy), and the architects of the Swedish welfare state, Gustav Möller and Gunnar Myrdal. Their ideas, built on the assumptions of gradualism and the neutrality of the state established previously, profoundly affected the party's understanding of socialism as well as its strategy for the realization of a socialist society in Sweden and would, in turn, form an essential part of the bedrock of SAP ideology decades later.

For Per Albin Hansson, the SAP's third leader (if Rickard Sandler's brief tenure as a replacement for Branting in 1925-26 is considered) and Prime Minister from 1932-46, the party's "essential task" was to organize Sweden's "socialist transformation process" (Therborn, 1984).[6] However, following the 1928 electoral setback the party suffered while campaigning on a somewhat more radical program (calling for the creation of a state bank, the nationalization of natural resources, and an extensive inheritance tax which would provide funds for socially-inspired capital investment projects), the party's election manifesto in 1932 did not address questions concerning nationalization or socialism. Hansson and other members of the Party

Executive felt that, in the context of the Depression, such questions should be put off. Emphasis at the policy level was instead placed on cautious social reforms. The reforms would allow for an alliance between the SAP and the Agrarian Party (unemployment insurance in 1934, a new pension plan in 1935, and so on) while the Commission on Socialization, established in 1920, was gradually dissolved between 1932 and 1935.

During this period, the supra-class idea that the SAP was really "a party of the whole nation," rather than solely a party of the working class, was effectively encapsulated in the idea of the "folkhem," or "People's Home," popularized and promulgated by Hansson. It was first introduced by Hansson in a famous 1928 parliamentary speech and explicitly evoked the image of Sweden as a family:

> The basis of the home is community and the feeling of togetherness. The good home knows no privileged or disadvantaged, no favourites and no step-children. There, one does not look down upon the other, there, nobody tries to get himself an advantage at the cost of the other, the strong one does not hold down and plunder the weak. In the good home there prevails equality, consideration, cooperation, helpfulness. Applied to the great people and citizens' home this would mean the breaking down of all social and economic barriers, which now divide the citizens into privileged and disadvantaged, into rulers and dependents, into rich and poor, propertied and miserable, plunderers and plundered (quoted in Therborn, 1984:573).

According to Seppo Hentilä (1978) the use of the folkhem concept should be seen as an important stage in the "breakthrough of reformism," in which the party attempted both to "abolish social class," and hence class conflict, and to introduce the idea that socialism could be achieved through social welfare reforms carried out by the state.[7]

Although he died an untimely death in 1926 at the age of thirty-three, Nils Karleby's work had a significant impact on the conceptualization of socialism within the SAP during this second stage. Indeed, Tage Erlander, Hansson's successor as party leader and Prime Minister from 1946-69, frequently referred to Karleby (and Ernst Wigforss) as the SAP's foremost theoretician and an important influence on his own thinking regarding socialism. Following the Swedish jurist Östen Undén, Karleby maintained that property should not be understood as an indivisible block of rights but as a "bundle of rights" which could be gradually socialized. For Karleby, social reforms -- factory legislation, the eight-hour day, accident and unemployment insurance, and so on - constituted a "socialist reallocation" of some of capital's rights concerning the profits distribution and workplace regulation, and he believed that a socialist society could be created through the continual curtailment of capital's rights in this manner (Tilton, n.d.). Out of step with some of his contemporaries during the 1920s, who called for nationalization, socialization and/or centralized economic planning, Karleby held that the market was much more efficient. His views played an important role in relegating the notion of formal, juridical ownership to a subordinate status, as well as in the party's acceptance of private ownership and the market. For Karleby, as well as Rickard Sandler who served as Secretary under his Chairship on the Socialization Committee in the early 1920s, the "critique of capitalism centred on the distribution of *property* and not on the workings of the *market*" (Tilton, 1987:150). As Prime Minister Erlander remarked, Karleby's approach thereby justified the SAP's daily reform work.

Perhaps the most pre-eminent, productive and formative theoretician in the SAP was Ernst Wigforss, the party's finance minister in the Branting cabinet of 1925-26 as well as during the critical period between 1932 and 1949. Outside of Sweden, Wigforss is primarily known for his policies in the 1930s, which are said to have anticipated the Keynesian revolution.[8] However, as early as 1919, Wigforss had drafted a program (the Gothenburg Program) which, although not adopted by the party, called for the socialization of finance and insurance and an extension of consumer cooperatives, in addition to a long list of more familiar "redistributive" reforms similar to that put forward by Bernstein in the Erfurt Program (Tilton, 1984). Within Sweden, Wigforss is widely associated with the introduction and defense of the idea of democratizing the economic sphere:

> Why should democracy be limited to political life? Why should it stop at industry and its hereditary control, when it did not stop at royal control and the hereditary aristocracy? That is difficult to teach the worker....He must ask himself if the private owners' tasks are so difficult that workers and employees could not learn to carry them out (quoted in Higgins, 1985a:218).

Like his contemporaries, Wigforss maintained that nationalization was not an end in itself but only one neither necessary nor sufficient means by which to begin to build a society based on socialist values: equality, democracy, freedom, security and solidarity. And, like Karleby, he held that the creation of such a society required only that the power held by capitalists be democratized, not that the capitalist class itself be eliminated. Economic planning could organize the economy for higher and more efficient production while undermining capital's monopoly over investment and production decisions (economic democracy); legislation could be implemented that would democratize the workplace (industrial democracy); social welfare policies and progressive taxation could create a more equitable distribution of national resources (Tilton, 1979; Wigforss, 1924). After his retirement as Finance Minister in the 1950s, Wigforss "repudiated the notion that affluence cured the ills of capitalist society" and called for the creation of "public enterprises without owners" as an alternative to state ownership (Tilton, 1987:163).[9]

The 1944 party program was clearly shaped by the work of Karleby and Wigforss. The further displacement of strategies calling for nationalization resulted from the SAP's acceptance of their ideas and its 1944 program declared that "the decisive feature of the bourgeois economy is not private ownership of property but that the *right of ownership* and the *right of determination* of the essential material means of production lie in the hands of a minority..." (quoted in Sainsbury, 1980:34). The SAP also adopted a second program in 1944, the 27-Point Post-War Program, which had been drafted by a committee composed of LO and SAP delegates and chaired by Wigforss. The tendency toward the attenuation of the idea of nationalization, even as a *means* of creating a socialist society, reached a peak in this program. Nationalization was viewed as almost completely subordinate to a strategy of economic planning, i.e., steering the capital market, regulating investment, boosting purchasing power, rationalizing the various branches of the economy, supervising foreign trade, and expanding cooperative and other non-profit production. However, while the SAP had largely abandoned its emphasis on nationalization, the programs it put forward in the 1940s were still radical in nature, due perhaps in part to its improved electoral fortunes as well as those of the VPK.[10]

By the 1950s the LO, which had previously had only a marginal influence on SAP policy, began to question some of the policies and to develop innovative policies from its own perspective, which the party was obliged to adopt (Therborn, 1986). The Rehn-Meidner model, for example, was its alternative to the SAP's incomes policy. The LO also produced its own proposal for a supplementary pension system. This marked the beginning of a more independent relationship between the SAP and the LO.

Functional socialism: the legacy of the past, 1960s to the present

Historically, nationalization has played a very minor role in Sweden. The late-nineteenth century witnessed the creation of a handful of commercial state agencies necessary to unify and defend a relatively undeveloped and sparsely inhabited country (the Telecommunications Board in 1853 and the

State Railways in 1862) and to develop and maintain domestic control over Swedish resources (the Forest Board in 1859 and the State Power Board in 1909). In the twentieth century, a number of state corporations emerged but they did not result from a program of nationalization either. Rather, they were created on an individual basis in response to some concrete and specific problems and were usually required to compete with private industry (Verney, 1959). Moreover, not all of them were created by the SAP. The Swedish Tobacco Monopoly (1915), for example, was formed by the Liberal government to meet the cost of its 1913 pension plan. The Wine and Spirits Company (1917) was established by a Conservative government to restrict liquor consumption. It was also a Conservative government that created the large iron-mining corporation, LKAB, in the early 1900s. The SAP did establish several industries while in power from 1932 to 1976, particularly between 1965 and 1975, but it actually nationalized relatively few existing private industries. In fact, amidst the economic crisis of the 1970s and early 1980s, the bourgeois coalition governments nationalized more private industry during the first three of their six years in office (1976-1982) than the SAP did throughout its entire forty-four year incumbency (Pontusson, 1988). While the Swedish state came to own directly or indirectly a significant number of companies (28), approximately 90 percent of Swedish industry remained in private hands with only about 6 percent controlled by the national government (Spybey and Lawrence, 1986; Törnblom, 1977).

Of course the fact that the SAP took control over relatively few financial, commercial or industrial enterprises in Sweden while in power, and gradually came to reject nationalization in favour of economic planning is not, in itself, necessarily an indication that the party was any less committed to socialism or some form of economic democracy. Wigforss had correctly pointed out that any strategy solely based on the socialization of key Swedish enterprises would only address those problems resulting from private property rights, not those occurring from the excessive reliance of those enterprises upon market mechanisms, and that such an approach would not lead to a more democratic workplace but to bureaucratization and other problems identified with "state capitalism." However, the SAP had also failed to carry out its alternative strategy, the institutionalization of economic planning. If not totally abandoned, the SAP's planning strategy was redefined. The original emphasis on investment steering gave way to a concern with coordinating the economy through long-term economic forecasting, collaboration with capital to promote economic growth and smooth out business cycles, and an expansion of the public sector[11] (Pontusson, 1986; Therborn, 1984).

While the SAP's failure to implement economic planning in the 1930s and its retreat from its radical, interventionist planning program in the 1940s can be partly accounted for by factors such as the Depression, electoral problems, the intense and vociferous anti-planning campaign launched by a united capitalist class and the bourgeois parties in the 1940s, and the still relatively weak power resources of the working class, it should also be remembered that the party itself had failed to translate its call for economic planning into concrete reforms and policy initiatives, relegating this task instead to various public commissions of inquiry where "business enjoyed a decisive advantage" (Pontusson, 1986:118).

With its radical planning strategy set aside, the SAP now became more concerned with organizing capitalism rather than transforming it. By 1960, the party program made little if any reference to class conflict and, following in the "folkhem" tradition, appealed to the *national interest* and to "vague and general categories of people," such as "citizens," "people," and "men" rather than to the "working class," the "exploited classes," or "workers," as in earlier programs (Helenius, 1969:39-40). According to Hamilton (1989:227), "the dissemination of the idea that the party is committed to the national interest [rather than that of the working class] must be part of the rhetoric of any party seeking to maximise votes in elections." This accepts the very narrow definition of the "working class" adopted by Przeworski (1980; also Przeworski and Sprague, 1986) - which under-estimates the size of the working class by including traditional "blue-collar" workers but excluding the myriad of lower echelon clerical, commercial, and other non-industrial "white-collar" workers. It absolves the leadership of a party theoretically committed to socialism or economic democracy of its responsibility to foster a working class identity among all workers, both "productive" and "non-productive."

The 1960 program also concluded that "through legislation and trade union struggles, the despotic power of private capitalists was broken" (quoted in Helenius, 1969:40). And, in contrast with earlier programs that called for "socialist production, planned on the basis of the real needs of the society," and aimed to "completely reform the economic organization of bourgeois society and carry through the emancipation of the exploited classes," this program simply stated that "economic planning must be directed towards maintaining full employment and a fair distribution of the goods produced while preserving a stable economy" (quoted in Helenius, 1969:69). The SAP's new commitment, at both the ideological and policy level, is best expressed by the concept of "functional socialism" introduced by Gunnar Adler-Karlsson (a social democrat and an assistant to Gunnar Myrdal) but obviously based largely on the work of Undén, Karleby, and, to a lesser extent, Wigforss:

> It is my conviction that much of the present ideological debate in terms of *socialism versus capitalism* is not only outdated but even outright dangerous as it blurs our deeper understanding of the ideological problems of our societies, and as it makes us less efficient in our fight for socialist ideas. The debate is still largely centering around the formal ownership, private or by the state, of the means of production. Actually, the formal ownership of the means of production is a secondary issue, as has been amply proved by Swedish socialist experience. What is of prime importance is the distribution in society of the economic and political functions which are hidden beneath formal ownership (Adler-Karlsson, 1970:1).

Following Karleby, Adler-Karlsson suggested in a widely quoted passage that by gradually "socializing" certain "functions" of private ownership, the power of capital would be decisively restricted and the SAP would be able to ensure both economic growth and a much fairer distribution of society's wealth while leaving industry in private hands:

> Let us look upon our capitalists in the same way as we have looked upon our kings in Scandinavia. A hundred years ago a Scandinavian king carried a lot of power. Fifty years ago he still had considerable power. According to our constitutions the king still has equally as much formal power as a hundred years ago, but in reality we have undressed him of all his power functions so that to-day he is in fact powerless. We have done this without dangerous and disruptive internal fights. Let us in the same manner avoid the even more dangerous contests which are unavoidable if we enter the road of formal socialization. Let us instead strip and divest our present capitalists of one after another of their ownership functions. Let us give them a new dress, but one similar to that of the famous emperor in H.C. Andersen's tale. After a few decades they will then remain, perhaps formally as kings but in reality as naked symbols of a passed and inferior development stage (Adler-Karlsson, 1970:95-96).

Embedded in the notion of functional socialism is the assumption that labour and capital share common interests and that capital will be more *willing* to share with labour if there is economic growth and higher profits. It also glosses over the fact that while certain ownership functions or rights can be regulated by degrees (the right to organize and control labour, the right to use the surplus-value of the labour of workers, and so on), others cannot (the right to buy the labour of workers, or the right not to use or even destroy capital). Moreover, Wigforss' and Karleby's emphases on industrial democracy and participation, respectively, were downplayed in this new formulation. In practice, functional socialism, despite the radical rhetoric, has essentially served as a means of rationalizing the SAP's reformist policies (Abrahamsson and Broström, 1980; Hamilton, 1989; Tilton, n.d.).

If the LO's policy development had become somewhat more autonomous from the SAP in the 1950s, this tendency continued over the next few decades. Although discussions of the wage-earner fund program often point to the "radicalization" of the Swedish "labour movement" in the late 1960s and 1970s, it is clear that it was the LO that was the source of this radicalism and not the SAP, which remained committed to functional socialism only. It is of some significance that it was the LO that discerned a number of problems with the Swedish model (such as stagnating levels of investment, the increasing concentration of wealth and power resulting from the "excess profits" created by the solidaristic wage policy, and the need for more democracy in the economy), and suggested an investigation of the feasibility of wage-earner funds as a possible solution. It is even more significant that Rudolf Meidner and his two research assistants from the LO, Anna Hedborg and Gunnar Fond, developed their proposal for wage-earner funds in complete isolation from, and without the knowledge of, the SAP executive. Moreover, at its June congress in 1976, the LO overwhelmingly endorsed the original, radical wage-earner fund program, suggesting only a few minor revisions (one of which actually made the Meidner Plan somewhat more radical by proposing that even small firms be included).

Of the 24 centrals belonging to the LO, it was those that organized industrial unions, rather than public sector unions, that were the most enthusiastic about the Meidner Plan (Edin, 1987). Of course the strongest support within the LO came from a relatively small group of approximately 18,000 trade union activists (1-2 percent of the LO membership) who had been involved in study circles throughout Sweden, discussing and debating the fund issue. A number of polls indicated that at least half the LO membership at large did not support the Meidner Plan (Kelman, 1977; Madsen, 1980). This disunity within the LO undoubtedly weakened the power position of labour regardless of the high levels of blue collar unionization and centralization which power resource theorists focus upon.

Despite the lack of unanimity within the LO, its understanding of economic democracy and the means by which it should be created differed profoundly from that of the SAP, even if both interpreted and were inspired by ideologues such as Wigforss. The ever-sharpening disagreements between these two bodies over economic democracy, as well as other issues, became known in Sweden as "the war of the roses." As one authority on political life in Sweden remarked, "never before did the two branches of the labour movement appear so divided in an electoral campaign, as they did in 1976" (Elvander, 1979:155).

For key strategists and party activists within the LO, having long largely abandoned the idea of nationalization and state ownership, economic democracy meant that the means of production would be owned and controlled by wage earners. The Meidner Plan was a means of moving Sweden in the direction of socialism:

> Wage earner funds contain an element of socialism in a very traditional sense. Socialism means that at least part of the means of production is transferred into the hands of the wage-earners as a collective....Social Democrats don't deal with the word socialism because they know people are afraid. For political reasons they avoid the term. But for me democratic socialism, in the sense of more influence for wage earners and the government over the means of production, is in the good Swedish tradition, the labour movement tradition. It is really nothing new and goes back to the ideas of Branting and Wigforss. So I am not the least unwilling to admit that there is an element of socialism in the original wage-earner funds (Meidner, 1987).

That the LO saw the wage-earner fund program as means of radically restructuring Swedish society along socialist lines was evident in an overly-optimistic and tactically disastrous headline in a labour newspaper, which proclaimed "now we shall take over."

While there was not an overwhelming amount of support for the Meidner Plan within the SAP, according to one poll about 24 percent of the membership of the party endorsed it (Madsen, 1980). The party leadership, which had just produced a traditional election campaign program that paid little attention to the idea of capital ownership, was much less enthusiastic. Both Kjell-Olof Feldt, the party's Finance Minister, and Prime Minister Olof Palme rejected Meidner's idea for wage-earner funds from the start but they attempted to bury the issue until after the election. Not only was it completely impractical and unworkable, in their view, but it would simply replace one dominant group (capitalists) with another (workers). Thus Feldt argues that the wage-earner fund program, which was finally implemented in 1983 should not be seen as a retreat because they party never supported Meidner's Plan:

> The idea of the Meidner Plan was to slowly strangle capitalism...What I tried to explain to my friends in the trade union movement was that this is practically impossible...My objections to the plan were very strong from the first time I saw it. I thought it was impossible to perform without changing the Swedish system into something quite different...The present funds don't break the neck of capitalism and they were never intended to do so as far as the party was concerned. They were not a retreat from the Meidner plan because it was impossible. We had to move away from the Meidner plan and create something that would work and be accepted by the people in democratic elections (Feldt, 1987a).

Other strategists within the party were also unhappy with the "syndicalist" nature of the Meidner Plan. They maintained that, as well as implying a difficult "double role" for unions, which would have to act as the representatives of workers and as owners, it would also lead to an incomplete form of economic democracy which would include capitalists and salaried managers while excluding pensioners, housewives, students and the handicapped. One party strategist, Walter Korpi (1978b, 1983), proposed a system of funds to be governed by all citizens in an attempt to deal with these problems. However, neither the SAP's Executive nor that of the LO was ready to back such a proposal. The latter continued to maintain that the emphasis had to be on the wage earner because one of the central goals of the Meidner Plan was to improve the situation of the worker. Citizen funds would give too much control to consumers who would be interested in other issues, such as lowering prices or raising productivity, which might contradict the needs of workers (Edin, 1987; Hedborg, 1987; Meidner, 1987). In addition, it would be the workers who were exchanging wage increases for shares. It should be clear from the foregoing that the SAP and the LO were not as one concerning the issue of economic democracy. If the Swedish labour movement was divided over the question of wage-earner funds, so too was the Swedish working class itself.

Disunity within the Swedish working class

As in a Catholic marriage, as Meidner colourfully pointed out, the political (SAP) and economic (LO) partners that constitute the Swedish labour movement remain stuck with each other no matter how bitterly they quarrel. The two major white-collar peak federations, TCO and SACO/SR, on the other hand, fall outside of the "labour movement" proper. Unlike the LO, the TCO has no formal links, past or present, with the SAP. Nor is it formally connected to the LO, although it has generally cooperated quite closely with it. However, as will be demonstrated, political developments eventually prevented the TCO from allying itself with the LO over the issue of wage-earner funds. The other, much smaller, white-collar confederation, SACO/SR, has not normally been supportive of LO or SAP programs and polices, and it adamantly opposed the wage-earner fund plan from the start, although its role in the debate was not nearly as pivotal as the TCO's.

The first white-collar organizations in Sweden were formed at the turn of the century but salaried employees were not extensively organized until the latter half of the century. This was relatively late in relation to their blue-collar counterparts in Sweden, although comparatively early by international standards. DACO, the central organization for private sector white-collar workers, was created in 1931, while its public sector equivalent, gamla (old) TCO was formed six years later. An amalgamation of these two organizations in 1944 led to the creation of TCO. SACO, the Swedish Confederation of Professional Associations (organizing associations of jurists, physicians, dentists, civil engineers, university professors, teachers and social workers) and SR, the National Confederation of Civil Servants (which organizes high-ranking civil servants and military officers), were created in 1947 and 1946 respectively and eventually merged in 1974 with a membership of well over 117,000, or about 4 percent of the Swedish work force (Heclo and Madsen, 1987; Heidenheimer, 1976). Unionization among white-collar workers in Sweden increased dramatically after the creation of these central bodies. Only about 25 percent of salaried employees were organized in the 1940s but, by the 1950s, white-collar unionization reached 50 percent and climbed further to approximately 75 percent by the 1970s (Korpi, 1978b). During this period, a successive series of Acts implemented in 1936, 1940 and 1966 ultimately granted all public sector employees (even those employed in police departments and the armed forces) rights of association and collective bargaining similar to those found in the private sector, including the right to strike (TCO, 1987).

By the 1970s, the TCO was firmly established as a central political and economic organization, in part reflecting a dramatic five-fold membership increase from 180,000 in the 1940s to approximately one million. However, it is predominantly an umbrella organization which, unlike the LO, does not engage in collective bargaining on behalf of its affiliates. Rather, white-collar unions belonging to the TCO negotiate with employers through three collective bargaining cartels, one for the state sector (TCO-S), one for the local government sector (KTK) and one for the private sector (PTK), as do those of SACO/SR.[11] And, although the TCO, as one of the most influential groups in Sweden, serves an important function as a pressure group for the policy aims of its white-collar workers, the individual unions "retain almost complete control over their organizational procedures, structures and viewpoints on policy issues" (Micheletti, 1985:41). This was not of minor significance during the struggle over wage-earner funds.

The most unique, and problematic, aspect of the TCO is its extreme heterogeneity. Comprised of twenty-odd industrially- or occupationally-organized federations, it encompasses a wide range of occupations and positions and a correspondingly wide range of income levels. The TCO is equally heterogeneous in terms of voting behaviour and the political sympathies of its membership. Support for political parties by TCO members covers the entire spectrum and, as with the Swedish electorate at large, is almost evenly divided between the socialist and non-socialist political blocs. As a result, the TCO is formally prohibited from supporting any of the political parties in any way. Of course the TCO's "political independence" does not prevent it from taking stands on important issues. However, when such issues become highly politicized, involving political partisanship and deep divisions between the various affiliates, the TCO becomes paralysed. This was demonstrated during the supplementary pension dispute in the 1950s as well as the wage-earner fund debate.

As pointed out above, the TCO is not formally linked to either the SAP or the LO. Of course the SAP's commitment to full employment, and the associated strengthening of bargaining power, makes a social democratic government attractive to the TCO. The TCO has cooperated with the LO since the early days of DACO in the 1930s and there has been a growing convergence between them on overall economic strategies in the past few decades (Martin, 1985a). But the TCO has often proven to be the more militant of the two organisations. This is reflected not only in higher levels of strike activity (or threats of strikes) among its affiliates, but by the fact that, except for the issue of wage-earner funds, it was the TCO, rather than the LO, that first initiated worker participation reforms. However, as Nils Elvander (1979:146) notes, in the early 1970s "there was an almost total meeting of the minds between the two confederations in their approach to industrial democracy."

The TCO first became seriously interested in wage-earner funds in the early 1970s, sparked by the discussions taking place within its sister organization in Denmark (FTF, the Danish Federation of Salaried Employees) as within the Liberal Party and the LO in Sweden (Nilsson, 1987). Like the LO, it created a research group to study the fund question and took part in the Royal Commission. It produced a preliminary report in 1972 (*Company Taxation and Wage-Earner Funds*), another in 1975 (*Wage-*

Earner Capital -- A Basis For Debate), and a third for its Congress in 1976 (*Wage-Earner Capital*), which were basically concerned with the same problems the LO had highlighted, although there was more emphasis on capital formation and a more equal distribution of wealth and less emphasis on economic democracy. And, like the LO, the TCO dismissed any proposals advocated by organized business or the bourgeois parties for individual profit-sharing, because they would serve to undermine the solidaristic wage policy, or for company-affiliated funds. The latter provided little attraction to those working in the public sector -- about 60 percent of all TCO members. The 1976 Congressional Report also stated that any fund scheme must include all employees, in both the public and private sectors, but did not present an actual proposal for a fund system. The report was approved as a basis for further discussion.

At its 1979 Congress, the TCO presented a new report (*Wage-Earner Capital -- A Proposal of Principles*). While not providing a detailed proposal either, it strongly supported the idea of wage-earner funds and collective ownership, even if the idea of capital formation was still central, and thus appeared to favour the joint LO-SAP fund proposal of 1978 (Karlsson, 1983; Micheletti, 1985; Öhman, 1984). However, by this time the TCO was already becoming highly factionalized as its various member associations, or fractions thereof, took sometimes diametrically opposed viewpoints on the fund issue and began to mobilize support for their positions.

In contrast with the situation in the LO, the public sector organizations were generally more supportive of the idea of wage-earner funds. The strongest support came from ST, the Federation of Civil Servants, one of the largest (with over 120,000 members) and most powerful of the TCO affiliates, and by far the most radical. Even if there was not unanimous support within this body, a majority of the ST membership expressed approval for wage-earner funds at the 1981 ST Congress. Moreover, while the LO had moved some considerable distance from its earlier proposals, the ST still supported the original Meidner Plan (Nyström, 1987). Lars-Erik Nyström, a research officer with ST, emphasized the fact that the ST leadership was much more active in mobilizing support for the funds than was the LO hierarchy, holding frequent meetings and discussions, and publishing newspaper articles and pamphlets while simultaneously attempting to counteract the anti-fund offensive launched by the business community and the bourgeois parties.

Within SIF, the Swedish Union of Clerical and Technical Employees in Industry, the largest and probably most powerful private sector federation (with well over 275,000 members) of all the TCO affiliates, a much greater degree of volatility and discord prevailed. Unable to properly "sound out" its membership and aware of some degree of disapproval for wage-earner funds, SIF's Executive Board had decided to recommend that its Congress refrain from taking a stand on the TCO's 1979 report, but a speech made to the SIF Congress by TCO's President, Lennart Bodström, convinced the Congress to vote against the Board's decision and support the TCO position. This move by Bodström was not without its consequences. SIF members opposing the idea of wage-earner funds and the 1979 report were outraged by this "outside interference" and began to assemble the forces of opposition within the federation, while the bourgeois presses criticized the TCO for trying to force its radical views on its member associations and circumvent democracy. When SIF's new position was sent to remiss referral -- a common consultative procedure by which proposals are circulated to interested parties for comment and criticism -- it was found that 70 percent of local SIF units and a clear majority of the membership did not support it. With a similar lack of support or outright opposition among most of the other TCO federations, the TCO could only again suggest that its report be used as a basis for continued work on the fund issue (Micheletti, 1985).

Despite the efforts of the leaders of SIF and TCO to promote the idea of wage-earner funds and encourage more discussion, the anti-fund elements within many of the TCO federations began to gain the upper hand over the next few years. Protest groups calling for an end to TCO involvement in, or at least a referendum on, the fund issue, emerged in ten different TCO federations (for example, SIF Members Against Wage-Earner Funds, Civil Servants Against Wage-Earner Funds, Bank Employees Against Wage-Earner Funds, Public Employees for Member Referendums on Wage-Earner Funds, Policemen For Member Referendums on Wage Earner Funds, and so on). In 1982, the groups united under a "peak" protest organization, TCO Members for Referendums on Wage-Earner Funds, to ensure a more effective anti-fund campaign. Another much smaller but very vocal protest group, TCO Against Wage-Earner Fund Socialism, also emerged during this period, although it had no direct links with any of the others. The various protest groups conducted polls among their sympathizers and financed surveys of the larger TCO membership by established pollsters. It used the polls to attempt to demonstrate that the TCO leadership was trying to push its own programs through without any regard for the membership viewpoint. They also took out full-page advertisements in the newspapers criticising the TCO and authored a barrage of articles in both the bourgeois and union presses attacking the TCO leaders and the fund idea.

For its part, the TCO decried the ability of fund opponents to "dig up" members from the TCO unions who had never before been involved in political or union issues:

> The fact is that these are people who have not earlier participated in union affairs and shows that they are not really interested in safeguarding the interests of wage earners. Only when they are asked by the conservatives, employer associations, and the non-socialist press to attempt to obstruct a union standpoint in favour of wage earner funds do they begin to show interest in union affairs (quoted in Micheletti, 1985:154).

In addition, one researcher at SIF noted that attempts to hold discussion groups to create interest in and promote wage-earner funds were often thwarted by middle-management, whose presence at these meetings intimidated the workers (Nygårds, 1987). As a result of all this, the TCO, at its 1982 Congress, was finally forced to adopt a neutral position, neither endorsing nor rejecting the idea of wage-earner funds. This move resulted not only from the tremendous disunity among and within the various TCO affiliates, but also reflected developments in the political sphere. While the Liberal Party was divided over the fund issue, there were key members in the Party, such as Ola Ullsten and Carl Tham, Party Leader and Party Secretary respectively, who were interested in reaching a compromise position on the fund question with the LO, TCO, and SAP. However, when the Party moved to the Right -- reflected in Ullsten's replacement as Party Leader and Tham's decision to join the SAP -- and a solid bloc of fund-opposition was created among the bourgeois parties, the TCO was formally bound to take a non-committal stand (Lendenius, 1987; Nilsson, 1987; Nygårds, 1987).

Despite their success in "neutralizing" the TCO, the protest groups continued to oppose wage-earner funds, taking part in the October 4th Demonstrations under their own banners both outside of Parliament and at TCO headquarters in 1983. While it has not been possible to substantiate claims that the various protest groups receive financial support from the business community, there can be no doubt that they have been positively received by the business community which has, in fact, published a book by one group's leading spokesperson, Gunilla Arhén (Micheletti, 1985). It is significant that when the SAP was awaiting remiss referrals from various interest groups before it made its decision to implement the final fund program in 1983, the TCO was unable to reply. Just as it did in the 1950s over the pension dispute, the TCO claimed that it needed more time. Meanwhile, the various protest groups had no trouble getting their message across, having submitted several remiss referrals for consideration by the SAP.

Conclusion

By narrowly focusing on the power resources of the labour movement, power resource theorists neglect other central factors that help account for the de-radicalization of the Meidner Plan, such as the ideological commitment of the Social Democrats and the degree of unity within the working class. It has been argued here that the SAP's ideology evolved through three stages. Its original commitment to creating socialism through nationalization gave way, in the 1920s and 1930s, to an emphasis on planning which, by the 1960s, developed into a concern with "functional socialism" only. The party was, therefore, ideologically out of synch with the LO's radical proposal for wage-earner funds. By the 1970s, the SAP and LO appeared much less like "branches from the same tree" than they had earlier.

The other major working class organization, the TCO -- structurally predisposed toward factionalization because of its extreme economic and political heterogeneity -- became markedly polarized both inter- and intra-federationally, while the SACO/SR was both united and unwavering in its opposition to the funds. Power resource theory's emphasis on the SAP's lengthy incumbency and the inordinately high levels of unionization in the Swedish work force indicate little about the party's goals and commitments and overlook the fractionalization and disunity within the Swedish working class, despite its very high level of unionization.

Notes

1. There are other accounts of the ideological development of the SAP besides those of Tingsten and Lewin. Knut Backström, for example, argues that the SAP abandoned its commitment to socialism because an opportunistic party leadership betrayed the working class, while Jan Lindhagen focuses on the effects of the depression and the threat of fascism as the central factors explaining why the party gave up its Marxist heritage. Unfortunately, neither of these accounts is available in English, but they are very briefly reviewed in Hentilä (1978) and Stephens (1981b).

2. The importance of examining the role of party ideology in discouraging non-reformist developments was demonstrated by Panitch (1971) with regard to the Labour Party in Britain.
3. One of the reasons the SAP lost power in 1926 was because it would not eliminate unemployment benefits for workers who refused to take jobs in factories where strikes were in progress.
4. These two terms are much more distinct in Swedish than they are in English according to Tilton (1987). While nationalization refers to state assumption of ownership, socialization is a much broader concept which encompasses a much wider range of ownership forms (cooperatives, syndicalist forms of organization and state ownership) as well as public control without ownership. The idea of autonomous public firms without ownership is one which the SAP borrowed from their Austrian counterparts according to Tilton (1987). Abrahamsson and Broström (1980:270) also suggest that Austro-Marxism "probably had a relatively large importance for Swedish social democracy." While ideas such as the possibility of using the existing state machinery to transform capitalist society and the notion of the "slow revolution" promulgated by central Austro-Marxists such as Rudolf Hilferding and Otto Bauer coincide with SAP ideology, there is, unfortunately, little evidence available in English to substantiate this claim (Tilton, 1989).
5. In the late 1920s, for example, the Socialization Committee dropped its plans to socialize the paper, electrical, and shoe industries.
6. Hansson was not Prime Minister for a brief three-month period in the summer of 1936 when the SAP-Agrarian government collapsed because the bourgeois parties would not agree to a revision of old-age and disability pensions.
7. Of course Hansson was not the first labour leader to make such supra-class appeals. As Panitch (1971:190) notes, the speeches of Ramsay MacDonald in Britain were "punctuated with a belief in the organic unity of society."
8. Don Patinkin (1982), alternatively, maintains that Wigforss, like a number of other economists, anticipated only *parts* of Keynes' theory.
9. "These enterprises would operate essentially as public foundations. They would pay a fixed interest on loans but would not issue shares. Their internal administration would feature industrial democracy; consumers might have representation on the firms' boards" (Tilton, 1987:163).
10. In the elections of 1940 the SAP won its first absolute majority, obtaining 53.8 percent of the votes. In the following election in 1944, the SAP's vote declined to 46.7 percent while that of the VPK climbed to 10.3 percent.

11. In addition to the Rehn-Meidner model and an elaborate welfare state, this included the creation of a state-owned bank in the late 1940s (Sveriges Kreditbank), a revised investment fund system in 1955 and the pension reform of 1959.
12. In competition for an overlapping constituency, the TCO and the SACO/SR are often at odds with one another. On several occasions bitter jurisdictional disputes have also arisen between LO-affiliated federations and TCO affiliates (see Lash, 1985).

5 Conclusion: The future of Swedish social democracy

An LO investigation into the performance of the wage earner fund program in 1987, three years after its implementation, could do little more than enthusiastically conclude that the dire predictions of catastrophe made by the fund's opponents had not been realized (LO, 1988; Meidner, 1987). Within the business community, however, it was widely held that labour might have won the *battle* over wage-earner funds but it had clearly lost the *war*. Nevertheless, owners of small businesses and industries remained adamant in their opposition to the existing system of funds and supported the Conservative Party's original suggestion (however unworkable) that all of the capital paid into the fund system be restored to the "rightful owners." Representatives of "big capital," alternatively, routinely refer to the wage-earner funds as "harmless," "meaningless," or "just another investor" but have continued to take part in "Fourth of October" demonstrations for ideological and symbolic purposes. The 1987 rally held in a large stadium in Stockholm, complete with clowns, jugglers, brassbands, dance bands and rock groups, attracted approximately 20,000 fund opponents from across the country (Dagens Nyheter, 1987a, 1987b). Over sixteen speeches from some of the directors and leading representatives of Swedish capital, including Curt

Nicolin (ASEA), Hans Werthén (Electrolux), Pehr Gyllenhammar (Volvo), and Gunnar Randholm, chairperson of the Fourth of October Committee (and managing director of Eldon), were delivered at this event. In addition to attacking the five regional wage-earner funds, they made it clear that capital would not tolerate *any* plans to further "socialize" the economy -- including the proposals then under discussion in labour circles to relax share restrictions on the existing four pension funds or to create a new share-purchasing "fifth" fund. Moreover, representatives of capital increasingly expressed their desire to break with the Swedish model (centralized wage bargaining, the solidaristic wage policy, and an extensive welfare state), and move toward a freer market (Carlsson, 1987; Grafström, 1988; Larsson, 1987). This new capital offensive reflects the growing imbalance in power between capital and labour in Sweden.

It has been argued here that labour's failure to implement its scheme to gradually democratize and socialize the Swedish economy through the creation of investment funds failed for two reasons, which power resource theorists fail to adequately address. First, a number of developments took place which dramatically increased the strength of capital. Accelerating levels of concentration and internationalization gave capital more leverage and decreased its dependence upon the domestic economy. These developments were actually encouraged by the SAP during the Social-Democratic Keynesian Era. Policy efforts (the solidaristic wage policy, taxation policies, the Investment Reserve Fund System, and centralized bargaining, among others) which sought to improve the lot of the working class and enhance its power resources by favouring the largest, most profitable corporations at the expense of the less-efficient and less-profitable industries, contributed to the high levels of concentration in Swedish industry and developed their export capacity. This greatly augmented the strength of capital. The fact that increases in labour's power resources were accompanied by, and indeed dependent upon, such increases in capital's power resources is a contradiction that power resource theory does not take into account.

Since these trends occurred within both home-market and export industries, capital also became much more unified. The gradual conversion of the largest and most profitable home-market manufacturers of raw materials into more "advanced" industries, or their elimination during the international economic crisis, and the increasing tendency for capital, home-market and export, to sell and, more importantly, to produce abroad, meant that capital could now more easily speak with one voice; that the various branches of industry could now collectively demand policies favouring an export orientation. This was reflected in the positions taken and the tactics used by the various business associations, especially SAF.

Labour reformism in Sweden had been possible partly because of an historical division between the home-market and export factions of capital, which the SAP was able to exploit. It was this potential for playing one faction of capital against another that allowed labour to make significant gains during the Social-Democratic Keynesian Era. Power resource theory cited only labour's increasing organizational power resources and its ability to forge alliances along class (farmers/blue-collar workers, blue collar/white collar workers) and political party (SAP/Agrarian, SAP/VPK) lines as the sole explanation. By the 1970s, however, that avenue was being closed as the factions of capital began to align. The threatening nature of the wage earner fund issue itself served to further obstruct that route by unifying capital.

These changes in the organization and unity of capital, which began to take shape in the 1950s and were accelerated by the onset of the crisis in the 1970s, have not abated throughout the 1980s and 1990s. Many of Sweden's wealthiest capitalists, such as Hans and Gad Rousing (Tetra Pak) and Ingvar Kamprad (IKEA), have recently emigrated and relocated their head offices abroad, thus evading Sweden's progressive personal tax system. Production abroad also allows such companies to avoid payments into welfare programs and the various funds (pension funds, renewal funds, wage-earner funds) as well as the progressive labour legislation passed in the 1970s. Sweden's large export industries have continued to expand through numerous mergers and acquisitions abroad, spurred on by the impending realization of the free internal market of the European Community in 1992. In the past few years, for example, Electrolux purchased Zanussi of Italy (1984), White Consolidated in the U.S. (1986), and Britain's Thorn EMI (1987). Volvo acquired Britain's Leyland Bus Group (1987), and ASEA merged with Switzerland's Brown Boveri (1987) in an attempt to gain "critical mass." In 1990 alone Stena purchased Sealink British Ferries, Svenska Cellulosa purchased the British paper manufacturer Reedpack, Stora, Europe's largest paper manufacturer, acquired the German conglomerate Feldmühle, and Nobel Industries bought up parts of the British paint company, Crown Berger. Indeed, by 1989/1990, Swedish firms were investing more capital abroad -- particularly in the European Community -- than in Sweden.

Financial deregulation brought on by the international crisis, which served to strengthen capital by weakening the power of the SAP over the capital market, has continued apace as well. Recent developments in the Swedish capital market include a host of new financial deregulations and innovations, including permission for foreign banks to conduct operations in Sweden

(1986), a 600 percent increase in the stock exchange index, and proposals to allow Sweden's banks to operate as merchant banks, making it much easier for them to acquire shares in their "customers" as of 1990. Klas Eklund, the special economic advisor to the Prime Minister, recently remarked that the changes currently underway in the Swedish financial market make London's Big Bang sound like a mere whimper (Economist, March, 1987).

As a result of the changes in the organization and unity of capital discussed above, the SAP has been policy-bound to play according to new rules in a new environment since its return to power in 1982. Once in office, the SAP, following the tactics of its bourgeois predecessors, immediately devalued the Krona by 16 percent to gain a larger share of the export market. This sent the profits of Sweden's large export industries into orbit while simultaneously leading to wage drift (undermining the solidaristic wage policy) and a decrease in real wages for workers, thus further decreasing labour's power.

The new political climate in Sweden is manifest not only in the exhaustive and aggressive ideological attacks made by the employers associations and bourgeois political parties on the wage-earner funds, but in the now commonplace demands for public sector cuts, decentralized wage bargaining and a "restoration" of the market. As a result of such demands and the constraints of an intensely competitive international capitalist market, the SAP was forced to backpedal on a number of issues. For example, it recently applied for membership within the European Community to both secure a market for Swedish products and stem the outflow of Swedish capital and the consequent drain on the balance of payments. It also postponed its planned shutdown of some of its nuclear power plants in response to capital's demands for cheap energy, dramatically lowered the maximum marginal rate of income tax and made some cuts to the public sector. Despite its efforts to borrow policies from its bourgeois political rivals, the SAP was unable to hold on to power in the recent election in September 1991.

The second reason dealt with here to account for labour's failure to transform Swedish capitalism was the degree of disunity and factionalization within the labour movement. By focusing only on organizational and political indicators of the power of labour, power resource theory assumes a much greater degree of unity within both the labour movement and the working class than actually exists -- particularly with regard to the idea of socialization and wage-earner funds. The creation or widening of ideological divisions between the LO and SAP, and the opposition to wage-earner funds expressed within the latter, was one indicator of the growing dissension within the labour movement as a whole, which was examined here in some detail. And it would seem that the prospects for the reunification of these bodies regarding such questions are dismal. While LO strategists continued to discuss proposals for wage-earner and pension funds as a means of gaining control over capital and maintain that the struggle over economic democracy is far from over (Edin, 1987), the lack of interest among the party executive within the SAP is readily apparent. At the SAP Congress in September 1987, the issue of economic democracy was relegated to a 2:00 A.M. discussion period which was far from lively and attended by only a handful of party members (Dagens Nyheter, 1987c). And, the SAP's leader, Ingvar Carlsson, and other key cabinet ministers such as Kjell-Olof Feldt and Anna Greta Leijon have publicly expressed their commitment to functional socialism only.

An attempt has been made here to provide account of the changing balance of power between capital and labour by supplementing power resource theory's focus on the increasing power resources of labour with an historical account of the development of capital's power and demonstrating the link between the power of labour and that of capital. One of the rather obvious conclusions that can be drawn from the present study is that the limits of Swedish social democracy are largely dependent upon the strength of capital. While labour's organizational and political power resources were sufficient to ensure substantial and meaningful gains for the Swedish working class, their efficacy in transforming Swedish capitalism was severely restricted. Moreover, it has been demonstrated that the balance of power between capital and labour is contingent upon economic conditions that can reverse or undermine both the reforms achieved by labour and its level of power.

A number of accounts of social democracy's failure to transform capitalism have focused on factors other than the balance of power between classes. Michels (1962), for example, maintained that those at the top of the necessarily oligarchical structure of all organizations, including social democratic parties, inevitably use their authority and control to carry out their own agendas, with little interference from the largely "passive and apathetic masses." Miliband (1972) also emphasized the role that party leadership, via its steadfast commitment to parliamentarism, has played in preventing social democratic parties from committing themselves to socialism. Przeworski's (1980) notion of electoralism also takes into account the party's commitment to parliamentary politics. He argued that, because the working class had failed to become a majority in capitalist society, it was unable to deliver an electoral victory to a social democratic or labour party. As a direct result, social democratic parties are forced to seek multi- or supra-class support, which has meant an abandonment of socialist goals.

Apart from its unnecessarily narrow identification of the working class with blue-collar workers, Przeworski's argument cannot account for the fact that, once in power, parties can and do pursue policies that are not supported by a majority of the electorate. Sven Steinmo (1988:437), for example, notes that the SAP struck a deal with the Agrarian and Liberal parties in 1980 "that, among other things, lowered marginal tax rates at the top end of the income scale at a time when 60 percent of the public were against lowering the rates on the rich." Moreover, all three of these accounts pay insufficient attention to the role of the working class and labour mobilization.

To a large extent, the examination of the rise and fall of the wage-earner fund plan and the limits of social democracy provided here has emphasized developments and contradictions largely external to the compromise reached between capital and labour. Marxist theories of corporatism, on the other hand, focus their attention on the contradictions that necessarily take place within the arrangements reached between capital and labour.[1] The centralization of authority within the labour confederations required by the solidaristic wage policy left unions with little control at the workplace; the solidaristic wage policy led to greater levels of inequality in power and wealth beyond the working class; managerial control in the workplace and worker participation on management's terms served to undermine the authority and legitimacy of the unions. However, such an approach is not incompatible with that taken here. Emphasizing the "systemic power" of capital, Marxist theorists of corporatism, while sometimes acknowledging labour strength as a precondition for corporatism, have argued that labour's attempts in the 1970s and 1980s to transcend the compromise it had reached with capital in the early decades of the Social-Democratic Keynesian Era, and with which it had become increasingly dissatisfied by the late 1960s, quickly discovered the limits of social democratic reformism.

While acknowledging the strength of power resource theory in accounting for the achievements of the working class *within* Swedish capitalism, it has been demonstrated here that the traditional concern of Marixst theories with the power and cohesion of capital must be brought back in. Strategically, this more inclusive examination of the balance of power between capital and labour in Sweden suggests that labour's ability to implement successfully system-transformative policies, like the original wage-earner fund plan, depends as much on the readiness of the SAP and the labour confederations to mobilize their memberships and the working-class in support of economic democracy as it does on the organizational and political power resources of labour.

Notes

1. Following Panitch (1986a:136), corporatism here refers to "a political structure within advanced capitalism which integrates organized socio-economic producer groups through a system of representation and co-operative mutual interaction at the leadership level and of mobilization and control at the mass level."

Appendix: Swedish governments since 1902

YEAR	PARTIES IN THE CABINET	PRIME MINISTER
1902-1905	Agrarian	Erik Gustaf Boström
1905-1905	Caretaker Government	Johan Ramstedt
1905-1905	National Coalition*	Christian Lundberg
1905-1906	Liberal	Karl Staaf
1906-1911	Conservative	Arvid Lindman
1911-1914	Liberal	Karl Staaf
1914-1917	Conservative	Hjalmar Hammarskjöld
1917-1917	Conservative	Carl Swartz
1917-1920	Liberal/SAP	Nils Edén
1920-1920	SAP	Hjalmar Branting
1920-1921	Caretaker Government	Louis De Geer
1920-1921	Caretaker Government	Oscar von Sydow

1921-1923	SAP	Hjalmar Branting
1923-1924	Conservative	Ernst Trygger
1924-1926	SAP	Hjalmar Branting
1926-1928	Liberal	Carl Gustaf Ekman
1928-1930	Conservative	Arvid Lindman
1930-1932	Liberal	Felix Hamrin
1932-1936	SAP	Per Albin Hansson
1936-1936	Agrarian	Axel Pehrsson-Bramstorp
1936-1939	SAP	Per Albin Hansson
1939-1945	Grand Coalition	Per Albin Hansson
1945-1946	SAP	Per Albin Hansson
1946-1969	SAP	Tage Erlander
1969-1976	SAP	Olof Palme
1976-1978	Centre, Moder., Lib.	Thorbjörn Fälldin
1978-1979	Liberal	Ola Ullsten
1979-1981	Centre, Moder., Lib.	Thorbjörn Fälldin
1981-1982	Centre, Liberal	Thorbjörn Fälldin
1982-1986	SAP	Olof Palme
1986-1991	SAP	Ingvar Carlsson
1991-	Centre-Right Coalition	Carl Bildt

* This Coalition did not include the SAP.

Note: The Liberal Party (Liberala Samlingspartiet) changed its name to the People's Party (Folkpartiet) in 1934. The Agrarian Party (Bondeförbundet) changed its name to the Centre Party (Centerpartiet) in 1958. The Conservative Party (Högerpartiet) changed its name to the Moderate Party (Moderata Samlingspartiet) in 1969. The SAP has held an absolute majority in parliament only three times - 1940-1942 (53.8% of votes), 1962-1964 (50.5% of votes), 1968-1970 (50.1% of votes).

Source: Hadenius (1985).

References

Interviews/personal communications

Åberg, Rune (1987). Professor of Sociology, University of Umeå, Sweden. November 26, Stockholm.
Carlsson, Bo (1987). Economist, SAF. November 20, Stockholm.
De Geer, Hans (1987). Director, Fa-Rådet (Swedish Council for Management and Work Life Issues). November 11, Stockholm.
Edin, Per-Olof (1987). Senior Economist and Head of Research Department, LO. Member of Ministry of Finance Committee that worked on 1983 Wage-Earner Fund Bill. December 1, December 11, Stockholm.
Erixon, Lennart (1987). Economist and researcher, Arbetslivcentrum. December 9, Stockholm.
Feldt, Kjell-Olof (1987a). Swedish Minister of Finance. Member of 1978 joint LO-SAP task force on wage-earner funds. Chaired 1981 LO-SAP task force on wage earner funds. December 22, Stockholm.
Gustafsson, Stig (1987). Legal Advisor to LO and TCO. SAP member. November 24, Stockholm.
Hedborg, Anna (1987). Senior Economist, LO. Assistant to R. Meidner in development of original wage earner fund plan. December 9, Stockholm.

Hermansson, Carl-Henrik (1987). Former leader of VPK (Swedish Communist Party), 1964-1975. Member of VPK Executive since 1946. December 16, Stockholm.

Larsson, Janerik (1987). Senior Vice President, SAF. Former Editor-in-Chief, SAF Tidningen. November 17, Stockholm.

Lendenius, Lars Gunnar (1987). Former Researcher, TCO. November 20, Stockholm.

Meidner, Rudolf (1987). Researcher, Arbestlivcentrum. Former Chief Economist, LO. "Father" of Meidner Plan. October 20, Stockholm.

Nilsson, Carl-Erik (1987). Director, TCO. Member of Royal Commission on Wage Earner Funds. December 17, Stockholm.

Nygårds, Peter (1987). General Secretary, SIF (Swedish Union of Clerical and Technical Employees in Industry - a TCO affiliate). November 25, Stockholm.

Nyström, Lars-Erik (1987). Former Research Officer, now Executive Assistant, ST (Federation of Civil Servants - a TCO affiliate) December 4, Stockholm.

Schager, Nils Henrik (1987). Researcher, IUI (Industrial Institute for Economic and Social Research). December 3, Stockholm.

Primary and secondary sources

Åberg, R., Selén, J., and Tham, H. (1987). "Economic resources." In R. Erikson and R. Åberg (eds), *Welfare in Transition: A Survey of Living Conditions in Sweden 1968-1981).* Oxford: Oxford University Press.

Abrahamsson, B. (1980). *Sweden: Industrial Democracy in the 1970's.* Stockholm: Arbetslivcentrum.

Abrahamsson, B. and Broström, A. (1980). *The Rights of Labor.* Beverly Hills: Sage.

Adler-Karlsson, G. (1970). *Reclaiming the Canadian Economy: A Swedish Approach Through Functional Socialism.* Toronto: Anansi.

Ahrne, G., Himmelstrand, U., and Lundberg, L. (1978). "'Middle Way' Sweden at a cross-road: Problems, actors, and outcomes." *Acta Sociologica, 21,* 317-340.

Aimer, P. (1985). The strategy of gradualism and the Swedish wage-earner funds. *West European Politics, 8,* 43-55.

Albinsson, G. (1967). "The metalworking industries." In M. Norgren (ed.), *Industry in Sweden.* Stockholm: The Federation of Swedish Industries.

Albrecht, S.L. (1981). "Preconditions for increased workers' influence." *Sociology of Work and Occupations, 8,* 252-272.

Albrecht, S.L. and Deutsch, S. (1981). "The challenge of economic democracy: The case of Sweden." *Economic and Industrial Democracy, 4,* 287-319.

Anderson, P. (1980). *Arguments Within English Marxism.* London: Verso.

Andersson, S.O. (n.d.). *The Swedish Labour Movement.* Stockholm: International Centre of the Swedish Labour Movement.

Apple, N., Higgins, W., and Wright, M. (1981). *Class Mobilisation and Economic Policy: The Struggles Over Full Employment in Britain and Sweden 1930-1980.* Stockholm: Arbetslivcentrum.

Arbose, J. and Skole, R. (1984). "The empire strikes back. *Sweden Now, 18,* 17-21.

Åsard, E. (1980). "Employee participation in Sweden 1971-1979: The issue of economic democracy." *Economic and Industrial Democracy, 1,* 371-393.

Åsard, E. (1986). "Industrial and economic democracy in Sweden: From consensus to confrontation." *European Journal of Political Research, 14,* 207-219.

Aspman, L.G. and Lundberg, E. (1985). A different business cycle pattern. *Skandinaviska Enskilda Banken Quarterly Review, 1,* 2-11.

Bergström, V. (1978). *The Political Economy of Swedish Capital Formation.* Stockholm: Arbetslivcentrum.

Bergström, V. and Södersten, J. (1984). "Do tax allowances stimulate investment?" *Scandinavian Journal of Economics, 86,* 244-268.

Berntson, L. (1979). "Post-war Swedish capitalism." In J. Fry (ed.), *Limits of the Welfare State: Critical Views on Post-War Sweden.* Westmead, England: Saxon House.

Björn, L. (1979). "Labour Parties, Economic Growth, and the Redistribution of Income in Capitalist Democracies." In R.F. Tomasson (ed.), *Comparative Social Research, 2,* 93-128.

Blake, D.J. (1960). "Swedish trade unions and the social democratic party: The formative years." *The Scandinavian Economic History Review, 8,* 19-44.

Blumberg, P. (1976). *Industrial Democracy: The Sociology of Participation.* New York: Schocken Books.

Bosworth, B.P. and Lawrence, R.Z. (1987). "Adjusting to slower economic growth: The domestic economy." In B.P. Bosworth and A.M. Rivlin (eds), *The Swedish Economy.* Washington: The Brookings Institution.

Bouveng, C. (1967). "Foreign trade." In M. Norgren (ed.), *Industry in Sweden*. Stockholm: The Federation of Swedish Industries.

Bowles, S. and Gintis, H. (1987). *Democracy and Capitalism*. New York: Basic Books.

Broström, A. (1986). Co-determination, work organisation, and the rights of labour. In J. Fry (ed.), *Towards a Democratic Rationality*. Aldershot: Gower.

Brym, R.J. (1986). "Incorporation versus power models of working class radicalism: With special reference to North America." *Canadian Journal of Sociology, 11,* 227-251.

Burkitt, B. (1983). Employee investment funds: A crucial element in the transition to socialism. *Economic and Industrial Democracy, 4,* 103-115.

Calmfors, L. (1985). "Exchange controls can be abolished!" *Skandinaviska Enskilda Banken Quarterly Review, 3,* 90-95.

Cameron, D.R. (1978). "The expansion of the public economy: A comparative analysis." *American Political Science Review, 72,* 1243-1261.

Cameron, D.R. (1982). "On the limits of the public economy." *Annals of the American Association of Political and Social Science, 459,* 46-62.

Cameron, D.R. (1985). "Social democracy, corporatism, labour quiescence and the representation of economic interest in advanced capitalist society." In J.H. Goldthorpe (ed.), *Order and Conflict in Contemporary Capitalism*. Oxford: Oxford University Press.

Carlson, B. (1969). *Trade Unions in Sweden*. Stockholm: Tiden.

Carnoy, M. and Shearer, D. (1980). *Economic Democracy: The Challenge of the 1980s*. Armonk, N.Y.: M.E. Sharpe.

Carnoy, M., Shearer, D., and Rumberger, R. (1983). *A New Social Contract*. New York: Harper and Row.

Castles, F.G. (1973). "The political functions of organized groups: The Swedish case." *Political Studies, 21,* 26-34.

Castles, F.G. (1975). "Swedish social democracy: The conditions of success." *Political Quarterly, 46,* 171-185.

Castles, F.G. and McKinlay, R.D. (1979). "Does politics matter: An analysis of the public welfare commitment in advanced democratic states." *European Journal of Political Research, 7,* 169-186.

Chandler, M. and Trebilcock, M. (1986). "Comparative survey of industrial policies in selected OECD countries." In D.G. McFetridge (ed.), *Economics of Industrial Policy and Strategy*. Toronto: University of Toronto Press.

Childs, M. (1947). *Sweden: The Middle Way.* New Haven: Yale University Press.

Childs, M. (1980). *Sweden: The Middle Way on Trial.* New Haven: Yale University Press.

Clegg, S., Boreham, P., and Dow, G. (1986). *Class Politics and the Economy.* London: Routledge and Kegan Paul.

Commission on Industrial and Economic Concentration (1976). "Ownership and influence in the economy." In R. Scase (ed.), *Readings in the Swedish Class Structure.* Oxford: Pergamon Press.

Cox, A. (1986). State, finance and industry in comparative perspective. In A. Cox (ed.), *State, Finance and Industry.* Brighton: Wheatsheaf Books.

Crick, B. (1987). *Socialism.* Minneapolis: University of Minnesota Press.

Cutright, P. (1965). Political structure, economic development, and national social security programs. *American Journal of Sociology, 70,* 537-550.

Dagens Nyheter (October 5, 1987a). "AP-Fonderna nästa stridsfråga."

Dagens Nyheter (October 5, 1987b). "Fondmotståndarnas dag."

Dagens Nyheter (October 6, 1987c). "Icke-debatt om ekonomisk demokrati."

Dahl, R.A. (1984). "Democracy in the workplace." *Dissent,* Winter, 54-60.

Dahl, R.A. (1985). *A Preface to Economic Democracy.* Berkeley: University of California Press.

Davies, R.J. (1979). "Introduction: Industrial democracy in international perspective." In G. Sanderson and F. Stapenhurst (eds), *Industrial Democracy Today: A New Role for Labour.* Toronto: McGraw-Hill Ryerson.

Dryzek, J. (1978). "Politics, economics and inequality: A cross-national analysis." *European Journal of Political Research, 6,* 399-410.

The Economist (March 7, 1987). "Sweden's economy: The nonconformist state."

The Economist (August 1, 1987). "Swedish multinationals: A hard act to follow."

The Economist (April 9, 1988). "Swedish takeovers: A European smorgasbord."

The Economist (June 23, 1990). "The Wallenberg Empire."

Eidem, R. and Öhman, B. (1979). *Economic Democracy Through Wage-earner Funds.* Stockholm: Arbetslivcentrum.

Elliot, J.E. (1987). "Karl Marx: Founding father of workers' self-governance?" *Economic and Industrial Democracy, 8,* 293-321.

Elvander, N. (1974). "In search of new relationships: Parties, unions, and salaried employees' associations in Sweden." *Industrial and Labor Relations Review, 28,* 60-79.

Elvander, N. (1979). "Sweden." In B.C. Roberts (ed.), *Towards Industrial Democracy: Europe, Japan and the United States.* Montclair: Allanheld, Osmun, & Co.

Engels, F. (1978). "The Tactics of Social Democracy (Engels' Introduction to Marx's The Class Struggles in France, 1848-1850)." In R.C. Tucker (ed.), *The Marx-Engels Reader.* New York: W.W. Norton.

Enström, P. and Levinson, K. (1982). *Industrial Relations in the Swedish Auto Industry - Developments in the Seventies.* Stockholm: Arbetslivcentrum.

Erikson, R. and Åberg, R. (1987). "The nature and distribution of welfare." In R. Erikson and R. Åberg (eds), *Welfare in Transition: A Survey of Living Conditions in Sweden 1968-1981.* Oxford: Oxford University Press.

Erikson, R., Goldthorpe, J.H., and Portocarero, L. (1982). "Social fluidity in industrial nations: England, France and Sweden." *British Journal of Sociology, 33,* 1-34.

Erixon, L. (1985). *What's wrong with the Swedish model? An analysis of its effects and changed conditions 1974-1985.* Stockholm: Swedish Institute for Social Research.

Erixon, L. (1988). Structural change and economic policy in Sweden during the post-war period. Unpublished manuscript, Arbetslivcentrum.

Esping-Andersen, G. (1978). "Social class, social democracy, and the state." *Comparative Politics, 11,* 43-58.

Esping-Andersen, G. (1979). "Comparative social policy and political conflict in advanced welfare states." *International Journal of Health Services, 9,* 269-293.

Esping-Andersen, G. (1980a). "The political limits of social democracy: State policy and party decomposition in Denmark and Sweden." In M. Zeitlin (ed.), *Classes, Class Conflict and the State.* Cambridge, Mass.: Winthrop.

Esping-Andersen, G. (1980b). *Social Class, Social Democracy, and State Policies.* Copenhagen: Nyt Fra Samfundsvidenskaberne.

Esping-Andersen, G. (1981). "From welfare state to democratic socialism: The politics of economic democracy in Denmark and Sweden." *Political Power and Social Theory, 2,* 111-140.

Esping-Andersen, G. (1985a). *Politics Against Markets: The Social Democratic Road to Power.* Princeton: Princeton University Press.

Esping-Andersen, G. (1985b). "Power and distributional regimes." *Politics and Society, 14,* 223-256.

Esping-Andersen, G. (1987a). "Citizenship and socialism: Decommodification and solidarity in the welfare state." In G. Esping-Andersen, M. Rein, and L. Rainwater (eds), *Stagnation and Renewal in Social Policy.* Armonk, N.Y.: M.E. Sharpe.

Esping-Andersen, G. (1987b) "The comparison of policy regimes: An introduction." In G. Esping-Andersen, M. Rein, and L. Rainwater (eds), *Stagnation and Renewal in Social Policy.* Armonk, N.Y.: M.E. Sharpe.

Esping-Andersen, G. (1989). "The three political economies of the welfare state." *Canadian Review of Sociology and Anthropology, 26,* 10-36.

Esping-Andersen, G. and Friedland, R. (1982). "Class coalitions in the making of West European economies." *Political Power and Social Theory, 3,* 1-52.

Esping-Andersen, G., Friedland, R., Wright, E.O. (1976). "Modes of class struggle and the capitalist state." *Kapitalistate, 4-5,* 186-220.

Esping-Andersen, G. and Korpi, W. (1984). "Social policy as class politics in post-war capitalism: Scandinavia, Austria, and Germany." In J.H. Goldthorpe (ed.), *Order and Conflict in Contemporary Capitalism.* Oxford: Clarendon Press.

Estrin, S. and Le Grand, J. (1989). "Market socialism." In J. Le Grand and S. Estrin (eds), *Market Socialism.* Oxford: Clarendon Press.

Euromoney (March, 1984). "Why Peter is different from Marcus."

Faxén, K. (1977). Planning, "fund socialism" and political democracy. *SAF Document No. 1095.* Stockholm: SAF.

Faxén, K., Odhner, C., and Spånt, R. (1988). The FOS Report - "A new model for wage formation." *Inside Sweden,* No. 2, 6-9.

Feldt, K. (1987b). "Sweden's third way is working." *Socialist Affairs,* No. 2, 42-45.

Fulcher, J. (1973). "Class conflict in Sweden." *Sociology, 7,* 49-70.

Fulcher, J. (1976). "Class conflict: Joint regulation and its decline." In R. Scase (ed.), *Readings in the Swedish Class Structure.* Oxford: Pergamon Press.

Fulcher, J. (1987). "Labour movement theory versus corporatism: Social democracy in Sweden." *Sociology, 21,* 231-252.

Fulcher, J. (1988a). "On the explanation of industrial relations diversity: Labour movements, employers and the state in Britain and Sweden." *British Journal of Industrial Relations, 26,* 246-274.

Fulcher, J. (1988b). "Trade unionism in Sweden." *Economic and Industrial Democracy, 9,* 129-140.

Gaitskell, H. (1939). "The banking system and economic policy." In M. Cole and C. Smith (eds), *Democratic Sweden.* London: George Routledge and Sons.

Gill, C.G. (1984). "Swedish wage-earner funds: The road to economic democracy?" *Journal of General Management, 9,* 37-59.

Glete, J. (1978). "The Kreuger Group and the crisis on the Swedish stock market." *Scandinavian Journal of History, 3,* 251-272.

Globe and Mail (May 9, 1988). "Richest Swedish Families Leave to Avoid High Taxes."

Goldthorpe, J.H. (1964). "Social stratification in industrial societies." In P. Halmos (ed.), The Development of Industrial Societies, *Sociological Review Monograph, 8,* 97-122.

Gourevitch, P. (1986). *Politics in Hard Times: Comparative Responses to International Economic Crises.* Ithaca: Cornell University Press.

Grafström, L. (1988). "Promoting employment in manufacturing: A Swedish employer's view." In G.M. Olsen (ed.), *Industrial Change and Labour Adjustment in Sweden and Canada.* Toronto: Garamond Press.

Graubard, A. (1984). "Ideas of economic democracy." *Dissent,* Fall, 415-423.

Greenberg, E.S. (1986). *Workplace Democracy: The Political Effects of Participation.* Ithaca: Cornell University Press.

Gustafsson, B. (1982). "Review symposium." *Acta Sociologica, 25,* 301-308.

Gustafsson, B. (1986). "Co-determination and wage earners' funds." In J. Fry (ed.), *Towards a Democratic Rationality.* Aldershot: Gower.

Gustavson, C.G. (1986). *The Small Giant: Sweden Enters the Industrial Era.* Athens, Ohio: Ohio University Press.

Hadenius, S. (1985). *Swedish Politics During the 20th Century.* Stockholm: The Swedish Institute.

Hall, P.A. (1984). "Patterns of economic policy: An organizational approach." In S. Bornstein, D. Held, and J. Krieger (eds), *The State in Capitalist Europe: A Casebook.* London: George Allen & Unwin.

Hall, P. (1986). *Governing the Economy: The Politics of State Intervention in Britain and France.* New York: Oxford University Press.

Hamilton, M.B. (1989). *Democratic Socialism in Britain and Sweden.* New York: St. Martin's Press.

Hammarström, O. (1987). Swedish industrial relations. In G.J. Bamber & R.D. Lansbury (eds), *International and Comparative Industrial Relations: A Study of Developed Market Economies.* London: George Allen & Unwin.

Hancock, M.D. (1972). *Sweden: The Politics of Postindustrial Change.* Hinsdale, Ill.: The Dryden Press.

Hancock, M.D. and Logue, J. (1984). "Sweden: The quest for economic democracy." *Polity, 17,* 248-270.

Hansson, S.O. (1984). "The challenge of big business." *Socialist Affairs, 2,* 43-45.

Headey, B. (1970). "Trade unions and national wage policies." *Journal of Politics, 32,* 407-439.

Heckscher, E.F. (1954). *An Economic History of Sweden.* Cambridge, Mass.: Harvard University Press.

Heclo, H. and Madsen, H. (1987). *Policy and Politics in Sweden: Principled Pragmatism.* Philadelphia: Temple University Press.

Hedborg, A. and Meidner, R. (1984). *Folkhemsmodellen.* Borås, Sweden: Rabén & Sjögren.

Hedborg, A. and Meidner, R. (1988). "The Swedish welfare state model." In G.M. Olsen (ed.), *Industrial Change and Labour Adjustment in Sweden and Canada.* Toronto: Garamond Press.

Hedström, P. and Swedberg, R. (1985). "The power of working class organizations and the inter-industrial wage-structure." *International Journal of Comparative Sociology, 26,* 90-99.

Heidenheimer, A.J. (1976). "Professional unions, public sector growth, and the Swedish equality policy." *Comparative Politics,* October, 49-73.

Helenius, R. (1969). *The Profile of Party Ideologies.* Stockholm: Svenska Bokforlaget.

Hellier, D. (1985). "Sweden's new boy network." *Euromoney,* April, 72-77.

Hentilä, S. (1978). "The origins of folkhem ideology in Swedish social democracy." *Scandinavian Journal of History, 3,* 323-345.

Hermansson, C. (1965). *Monopol och Storfinans - De 15 Familjerna (Monopoly and Big Business - The 15 Families).* Stockholm: Rabén & Sjögren.

Hermansson, C. (1987). "Swedish capital: National and international." Paper presented at the Symposium on the Swedish Model, Athens.

Hewitt, C. (1977). "The effect of political democracy and social democracy on equality in industrial societies: A cross-national comparison." *American Sociological Review, 42,* 450-464.

Hibbs, D.A. (1976). "Industrial conflict in advanced industrial societies." *American Political Science Review, 70,* 1033-1058.

Hibbs, D.A. (1977). "Political parties and macroeconomic policy." *American Political Science Review, 71,* 1467-1487.

Hibbs, D.A. (1978). "On the political economy of long-run trends in strike activity." *British Journal of Political Science, 8,* 153-175.

Higgins, W. (1980). "Working-class mobilization and socialism in Sweden: Lessons from afar." In P. Boreham and G. Dow (eds), *Work and Inequality,* Volume 1. Melbourne: Macmillan.

Higgins, W. (1985a). "Ernst Wigforss: The renewal of social democratic theory and practice." *Political Power and Social Theory, 5,* 207-250.

Higgins, W. (1985b). "Political unionism and the corporatist thesis." *Economic and Industrial Democracy, 6,* 349-381.

Higgins, W. (1986). "Industrial democracy and the control issue in Sweden." In E. Davis and R. Lansbury (eds), *Democracy and Control in the Workplace.* Melbourne: Longman Cheshire.

Higgins, W. and Apple, N. (1983). "How limited is reformism? A critique of Przeworski and Panitch." *Theory and Society, 12,* 603-630.

Himmelstrand, U. (1981a). "Spontaneity and planning in 'mixed economies' and under self-managing labour - with an inquiry into a Swedish proposal on wage-earners funds." In U. Himmelstrand (ed.), *Spontaneity and planning in social development.* London: Sage Publications.

Himmelstrand, U. (1981b). "Sweden: Paradise in trouble." In B. Denitch (ed.), *Democratic Socialism: The Mass Left in Advanced Industrial Societies.* Montclair: Allanheld, Osmun & Co.

Himmelstrand, U. (1983). "Sweden: Toward economic democracy." *Dissent,* Summer, 329-336.

Himmelstrand, U., Ahrne, G., Lundberg, L., and Lundberg, L. (1981). *Beyond Welfare Capitalism.* London: Heinemann.

Hodgson, G. (1984). *The Democratic Economy: A New Look at Planning, Markets and Power.* New York: Penguin Books.

Hollingsworth, J.R. and Hanneman, R.A. (1982). "Working-class power and the political economy of western capitalist societies." *Comparative Social Research, 5,* 61-80.

Holtback, R. (1988). "The production philosophy at Volvo." Speech presented at Sweden Works Seminar, Detroit, Michigan, April.

Hörnell, E. and Vahlne, J. (1986). *Multinationals: The Swedish Case.* London: Croom Helm.

Horvat, B. (1980). "Ethical foundations of self-government." *Economic and Industrial Democracy, 11,* 1-20.

Hufford, L. (1977). *Sweden's Power Elite.* Washington: University of America Press.

Hufford, L. (1973). "Sweden: The myth of socialism." *Young Fabian Pamphlet No. 33.* London: Fabian Society.

Ingham, G.K. (1974). *Strikes and Industrial Conflict: Britain and Scandinavia.* London: Macmillan.

Isaksson, M. and Skog, R. (1987). Ownership and control in large Swedish corporations (Preliminary draft). Stock Ownership and Efficiency Commission, Ministry of Industry, Stockholm.

Israel, J. (1974). "The welfare state - A manifestation of late capitalism." *Acta Sociologica, 17,* 310-329.

Israel, J. (1978). "Swedish socialism and big business." *Acta Sociologica, 21,* 341-353.

Jackson, T. (n.d.). *Worker ownership and economic democracy.* Ottawa: Canadian Centre for Policy Alternatives.

Jackson, P. and Sisson, K. (1976). "Employers' confederations in Sweden and the U.K. and the significance of industrial infrastructure." *British Journal of Industrial Relations, 14,* 306-323.

Jagrén, L. (1986). Concentration, exit, entry and reconstruction of Swedish manufacturing. In G. Eliasson (ed.), *The Economics of Institutions and Markets: IUI Yearbook 1986-1987.* Stockholm: The Industrial Institute for Economic and Social Research.

Jakobsson, U. (1986). "Economic growth in Sweden." In J. Sargent (Research Coordinator), *Foreign Macro-Economic Experience: A Symposium.* Toronto: University of Toronto Press.

Jessop, B. (1983a). "Accumulation strategies, state forms, and hegemonic projects." *Kapitalistate, 10-11,* 89-111.

Jessop, B. (1983b). "The capitalist state and the rule of capital: Problems in the analysis of business associations." *West European Politics, 6,* 139-162.

Johnston, T.L. (1962). *Collective Bargaining in Sweden.* London: George Allen & Unwin.

Johnston, T.L. (1977). "The Swedish employers' conference holds its first congress." *IR Research Reports, 2,* 8-10.

Johnston, T.L. (1981). "Sweden." In E.O. Smith (ed.), *Trade Unions in the Developed Economies.* London: Croom Helm.

Jonung, L. (1986). "Financial deregulation in Sweden." *Skandinaviska Enskilda Banken Quarterly review, 4,* 109-119.

Kapstein, J. (1988). "Peter Wallenberrg - Catalyst of Swedish industry." *Scandinavian Review, 76,* 16-25.

Karlsson, G. (1983). "Trade unions and collective capital formation." Brussels: European Trade Union Institute.

Kelly, J. (1988). *Trade Unions and Socialist Politics.* London: Verso.

Kelman, S. (1977). "Swedish elections - A test for socialism?" *Dissent, 24,* 138-140.

Kerr, C. et al. (1964). *Industrialism and Industrial Man.* New York: Oxford University Press.

Kolakowski, L. (1985). *Main Currents of Marxism 2: The Golden Age.* Oxford: Oxford University Press.

Korpi, W. (1978a). "Social democracy in welfare capitalism - structural erosion, welfare backlash and incorporation?" *Acta Sociologica,* Supplement, 97-111.

Korpi, W. (1978b). *The Working Class in Welfare Capitalism: Work, Unions and Politics in Sweden.* London: Routledge & Kegan Paul.

Korpi, W. (1980a). "Industrial relations and industrial conflict: The case of Sweden." In B. Martin and E. M. Kassalow (eds), *Labor Relations in Advanced Industrial Societies, Issues and Problems.* Washington: Carnegie Endowment for International Peace.

Korpi, W. (1980b). "Social policy and distributional conflict in the capitalist democracies. A preliminary comparative framework." *West European Politics, 3,* 296-316.

Korpi, W. (1981). "Sweden: Conflict, power and politics in industrial relations." In P.B. Doeringer with P. Gourevitch, P. Lange, and A. Martin (eds), *Industrial Relations in International Perspective: Essays on Research and Policy.* London: Macmillan.

Korpi, W. (1982). "The historical compromise and its dissolution." In B. Rydén and V. Bergström (eds), *Sweden: Choices for the 1980s.* London: George Allen & Unwin.

Korpi, W. (1983). *The Democratic Class Struggle.* London: Routledge & Kegan Paul.

Korpi, W. (1985a). "Economic growth and the welfare state: A comparative study of 18 OECD countries." *Labour and Society, 10,* 195-209.

Korpi, W. (1985b). "Economic growth and the welfare system: Leaky bucket or irrigation system?" *European Sociological Review, 1,* 97-118.

Korpi, W. (1985c). "Power resources approach vs. action and conflict: On causal and intentional explanation in the study of power." *Sociological Theory, 3,* 31-45.

Korpi, W. and Shalev, M. (1979). "Strikes, industrial relations and class conflict in capitalist societies." *British Journal of Sociology, 30,* 164-186.

Korpi, W. and Shalev, M. (1980). "Strikes, power, and politics in the western nations, 1900-1976." *Political Power and Social Theory, 1,* 301-334.

Kurzer, P. (1987). Conflict and cooperation: The role of capital in industrial politics in Belgium, the Netherlands, and Sweden. Unpublished doctoral dissertation, Rutgers, The State University of New Jersey.

Kuttner, B. (1983). Sweden/Denmark: Trials of Two Welfare States. *Atlantic Monthly*, 252, 14-22.

Landauer, C. (1959a). *European Socialism: A History of Ideas and Movements Volume 1.* Berkeley: University of California Press.

Landauer, C. (1959b). *European Socialism: A History of Ideas and Movements Volume 2.* Berkeley: University of California Press.

Lappé, F.M. (1983). "Sweden's Third Way to Worker Ownership." *The Nation*, February 19.

Larsson, J. (1987). *Turning Point.* Stockholm: Timbro.

Lash, S. (1985). "The end of neo-corporatism?: The breakdown of centralised bargaining in Sweden." *British Journal of Industrial Relations*, 23, 215-239.

Lash, S. and Urry, J. (1987). *The End of Organized Capitalism.* Cambridge: Polity Press.

Lawrence. P. and Spybey, T. (1986). *Management and Society in Sweden.* London: Routledge and Kegan Paul.

Laxer, G. (1981). The social origins of Canada's branch plant economy, 1837-1914. Unpublished Doctoral Dissertation, University of Toronto.

Laxer, G. (1989). *Open for Business: The Roots of Foreign Ownership in Canada.* Toronto: Oxford University Press.

Leibfried, S. (1978). "Public assistance in the United States and the Federal Republic of Germany: Does social democracy make a difference?" *Comparative Politics*, 11, 59-76.

Leion, A. (1985). "Employers' organizations." In B.C. Roberts (ed.), *Industrial Relations in Europe: The Imperatives of Change.* Sydney: Croom Helm.

Lenin, V.I. (1976). *The State and Revolution.* Peking: Foreign Languages Press.

Lenin, V.I. (1982). *Imperialism, the Highest Stage of Capitalism.* Moscow: Progress Publishers.

Lenin, V.I. (1983). *What Is To Be Done?* Moscow: Progress Publishers.

Levinson, C. (ed.), (1974). *Industry's Democratic Revolution.* London: George Allen & Unwin.

Lewin, L. (1975). "The debate on economic planning in Sweden." In Koblik, S. (ed.), *Sweden's Development from Poverty to Affluence, 1750-1970.* Minneapolis, University of Minnesota press.

Liebman, M. (1986). "Reformism Yesterday and Social Democracy Today." *Socialist Register, 1985/86,* 1-22.

Lindbeck, A. (1976). "Wage earner funds." Translated in *Document No. 1446.* Stockholm: SAF.

Lindeman, A.S. (1983). *A History of European Socialism.* New Haven: Yale University Press.

Lindhagen, J. (1979). "A sociology that politicizes." *Acta Sociologica, 22,* 289-292.

Lipset, S.M. (1983). *Political Man.* Baltimore: The Johns Hopkins University Press.

Ljunggren, O. (1980). "The role of employers organizations in politics and the formation of public opinion." *SAF Document No. 1094:I.* Stockholm: SAF.

LO (1953). *Trade Unions and Full Employment.* Stockholm: LO.

LO (1976). *Wage-earner Investment Funds.* Stockholm: LO.

LO (1982a). *Co-Determination Through Collective Agreements and Legislation.* Stockholm: LO.

LO (1982b). *The Labour Movement and Employee Investment Funds.* Stockholm: LO.

LO (1988). *3 Years with Employee Investment Funds: An Evaluation.* Stockholm: LO.

Luxemburg, R. (1982). *Reform or Revolution.* New York: Pathfinder Press.

Lyon, V. (1985). "Citizen funds." *Policy Options Politiques.* January, 23-26.

Lyon, V. (1986). Swedish Wage Earner Funds: A Glimpse of Our Future? *Canadian Journal of Political Science, XIX:3,* 573-583.

Madsen, H.J. (1980). "Class power and participatory equality: Attitudes towards economic democracy in Denmark and Sweden." *Scandinavian Political Studies, 3,* 277-298.

Markovits, A.S. (1986). "German social democracy." *Studies in Political Economy, 19,* 83-112.

Martin, A. (1975a). "Is democratic control of capitalist economies possible?" In L. Lindberg, R. Alford, C. Crouch, and C. Offe (eds), *Stress and Contradiction in Modern Capitalism.* Lexington, Ma.: Lexington Books.

Martin A. (1975b). "Labour movement parties and inflation: Contrasting responses in Britain and Sweden." *Polity, 7,* 427-451.

Martin, A. (1977). "Sweden: Industrial democracy and social democratic strategy." In G.D. Garson (ed.), *Worker Self-Management in Industry: The West European Experience.* New York: Praeger.

Martin, A. (1979a). "The dynamics of change in a Keynesian political economy: The Swedish case and its implications." In C. Crouch (ed.), *State and Economy in Contemporary Capitalism*. London: Croom Helm.

Martin, A. (1979b). "From joint consultation to joint decision making: The re-distribution of workplace power in Sweden." In J.A. Fry (ed.), *Industrial Democracy and Labour Market Policy in Sweden*. Oxford: Pergamon Press.

Martin, A. (1981). "Economic stagnation and social stalemate in Sweden." In U.S. Congress, Joint Economic Committee, *Monetary Policy, Selective Credit Policy, and Industrial Policy in France, Britain, West Germany, and Sweden*. Staff Study, June 26, 1981, 97th Cong., 1st session.

Martin, A. (1985a). "Trade unions in Sweden: Strategic responses to change and crisis." In P. Gourevitch, A. Martin, G. Ross, C. Allen, S. Bornstein, and A. Markovitz (eds), *Unions and Economic Crisis: Britain, West Germany and Sweden*. London: George Allen & Unwin.

Martin, A. (1985b). "Wages, profits, and investment in Sweden." In L. Lindberg and C.S. Maier (eds), *The Politics of Inflation and Economic Stagnation*. Washington: The Brookings Institution.

Martin, A. (1987a). "The end of the 'Swedish Model?' Recent development in Swedish industrial relations." *Bulletin of Comparative Labour Relations, 16*, 93-128.

Martin, A. (1987b). "Unions, the quality of work, and technological change in Sweden." In C. Sirianni (ed.), *Worker Participation and the Politics of Reform*. Philadelphia: Temple University Press.

Martin, A. and Ross, G. (1980). "European trade unions and economic crisis: Perceptions and strategies." In J. Hayward (ed.), *Trade unions and politics in Western Europe*. London: F. Cass.

Marx, K. (1977). *Capital Volume I*. (Trans. Ben Fowkes). New York: Vintage.

Marx, K. (1978). "The possibility of non-violent revolution." In R.C. Tucker (ed.), *The Marx-Engels Reader*. New York: Norton.

McLellan, D. (1979). *Marxism After Marx*. London: Macmillan.

Meidner, R. (1974). *Co-ordination and Solidarity. An Approach to Wages Policy*. Stockholm: Prisma.

Meidner, R. (1978). *Employee Investment Funds: An Approach to Collective Capital Formation*. London: George Allen & Unwin.

Meidner, R. (1980a). "Capital formation through employee investment funds: A Swedish proposal." In B. Martin & E.M. Kassalow (eds), *Labor Relations in Advanced Industrial Societies: Issues and Problems*. Washington: Carnegie Endowment for International Peace.

Meidner, R. (1980b). "Our concept of the third way: Some remarks on the socio-political tenets of the Swedish labour movement." *Economic and Industrial Democracy, 1,* 343-369.

Meidner, R. (1981). "Collective asset formation through wage-earner funds." *International Labour Review, 120,* 303-317.

Meyerson, P. (1979). "Capital accumulation and ownership structure in Swedish industry: The employee fund debate in perspective." *Working Life in Sweden, 10,* 1-8.

Micheletti, M. (1985). Organizing interest and organized protest. Difficulties of member representation for the Swedish central organization of salaried employees (TCO). Unpublished doctoral dissertation, University of Stockholm.

Michels, R. (1962). *Political Parties.* New York: The Free Press.

Miliband, R. (1972). *Parliamentary Socialism.* London: Allen and Unwin.

Miliband, R. (1978). *Marxism and Politics.* Oxford: Oxford University Press.

Miliband, R. (1982). *Capitalist Democracy in Britain.* Oxford: Oxford University Press.

Miliband, R. (1983). The limitations of social democracy. Paper presented at The Marxist Centenary Conference, Winnipeg.

Miliband, R. and Liebman, M. (1986). "Beyond Social Democracy." *Socialist Register, 1985/86,* 476-489.

Milner, H. (1989). *Sweden: Social Democracy in Practice.* Oxford: Oxford University Press.

Ministry of Finance (1984). *Employee Investment Funds.* Stockholm: Ministry of Finance.

Ministry of Labour (1985). *The Swedish Act on Co-Determination at Work.* Stockholm: Ministry of Labour.

Montgomery, A. (1939). *The Rise of Modern Industry in Sweden.* London: P.S. King & Son.

Myhrman, J. and Sundberg, J. (1986). The credit market in transformation. *Skandinaviska Enskilda Banken Quarterly Review, 2,* 30-38.

Myrdal, H. (1981). "Collective wage-earner funds in Sweden: A road to socialism and the end of freedom of association." *International Labour Review, 120,* 319-334.

Navarro, V. (1983). "The determinants of social policy. A case study: Regulating health and safety at the workplace in Sweden." *International Journal of Health Services, 13,* 517-561.

O'Connor, J. (1988). "Covergence or divergence?: Change in welfare effort in OECD countries 1960-1980." *European Journal of Political Research, 16,* 277-299.

O'Connor, J. (1989). "Welfare expenditure and policy orientation in Canada in comparative perspective." *Canadian Review of Sociology and Anthropology, 26,* 127-150.

OECD (1981). *Regulations Affecting International Banking Operations.* Paris: OECD.

OECD (1982). *Controls on International Capital Movements.* Paris: OECD.

Offe, C. and Wiesenthal, H. (1980). "Two logics of collective action: Theoretical notes on social class and organizational form." *Political Power and Social Theory, 1,* 67-115.

Öhman, B. (1983). "The debate on wage-earner funds in Scandinavia." In C. Crouch and F.A. Heller (eds), *Organizational Democracy and Political Processes.* Chichester, N.Y.: John Wiley and Sons.

Öhman, B. (1984). Wage-earner funds: Background, problems, and possibilities. *Economic and Industrial Democracy, 1,* 417-432.

Olsen, E. (1984). "The dilemma of the social-democratic labor parties." *Daedalus, 113,* 169-194.

Olsen, G. (1988). "Unemployment and labour market policy in Sweden and Canada: An introduction." In G. Olsen (ed.), *Industrial Change and Labour Adjustment in Sweden and Canada.* Toronto: Garamond Press.

Palme, O. (1975). "Balancing jobs, investment, and democracy." *Business Week,* December 22.

Panitch, L. (1980). "Recent theorizations of corporatism: Reflections on a growth industry." *British Journal of Sociology, 31,* 159-187.

Panitch, L. (1981). "Trade unions and the capitalist state." *New Left Review, 125,* 21-43.

Panitch, L. (1971). "Ideology and integration: The case of the British labour party." *Political Studies, 19,* 184-200.

Panitch, (1986a). "The development of corporatism in liberal democracies." In L. Panitch, *Working Class Politics in Crisis: Essays on Labour and the State.* London: Verso.

Panitch, L. (1986b). "The Impasse of Social Democratic Politics." *Socialist Register, 1985/86,* 50-97.

Panitch, L. (1986c). "Social contract or socialism?" In J. Richards and D. Kerr (eds), *Canada, What's Left?* Edmonton: NeWest Publishers.

Panitch, L. (1986d). "The tripartite experience." In K. Banting (Research Co-ordinator), *The State and Economic Interests.* Toronto: University of Toronto Press.

Patinkin, D. (1982). *Anticipations of the General Theory?* Chicago: University of Chicago Press.

Parkin, F. (1971). *Class, Inequality and Political Order.* London: MacGibbon and Kee.

Pateman, C. (1970). *Participation and Democratic Theory.* London: Cambridge University Press.

Pestoff, V. (1983). "Dilemma facing Swedish consumer co-operatives; can members, markets, authorities and employees all be optimised?" In C. Crouch and F. Heller (eds), *Organizational Democracy and Political Processes.* Chichester, N.Y.: John Wiley and Sons.

Pontusson, J. (1983). "Comparative political economy of advanced capitalist states: Sweden and France." *Kapitalistate, 10-11,* 43-73.

Pontusson, J. (1984a). "Behind and beyond social democracy in Sweden." *New Left Review, 143,* 69-96.

Pontusson, J. (1984b). *Public Pension Funds and the Politics of Capital Formation in Sweden.* Stockholm: Arbetslivcentrum.

Pontusson, J. (1986). Labor reformism and the politics of capital formation in Sweden. Unpublished doctoral dissertation, University of California.

Pontusson, J. (1987a). "Radicalization and retreat in Swedish social democracy." *New Left Review, 165,* 5-33.

Pontusson, (1987b). "Sweden." In M. Kesselman and J. Krieger (eds), *European Politics in Transition.* Toronto: D.C. Heath & Co.

Pontusson, J. (1988). "The triumph of pragmatism: Nationalisation and privatisation in Sweden." *West European Politics, 11,* 129-145.

Poulantzas, N. (1978a). *Political Power and Social Classes.* London: Verso.

Poulantzas, N. (1978b). *State, Power, Socialism.* London: Verso.

Przeworski, A. (1980). Social democracy as a historical phenomenon. *New Left Review, 122,* 27-58.

Przeworski, A. and Sprague, J. (1986). *Paper Stones: A History of Electoral Socialism.* Chicago: University of Chicago Press.

Ramsay, H. and Haworth, N. (1984). "Worker capitalists? Profit-sharing, capital-sharing and juridical forms of socialism." *Economic and Industrial Democracy, 5,* 295-324.

Regini, M. and Esping-Andersen, G. (1980). "Trade union strategies and social policy in Italy and Sweden." *West European Politics, 3,* 107-123.

Rehn, G. (1952). "The problem of stability: An analysis and some policy proposals." In R. Turvey (ed.), *Wages Policy under Full Employment*. London: William Hodge.

Rehn, G. (1983). *The debate on employees' capital funds in Sweden*. Paper prepared for the Commission of the European Communities, Aug. 1983, Brussels.

Richardson, P. (1982). *Wage-Earner Funds: The Evolution of an Idea*. Stockholm: Arbetslivcentrum.

Rinehart, J.W. (1987). *The Tyranny of Work: Alienation and the Labour Process*. Toronto: Harcourt Brace Jovanovich.

Ritzer, G. (1977). *Working: Conflict and Change*. Englewood Cliffs: Prentice-Hall.

Rock, C. (1986). Economic democracy and Sweden: Economic thought, institutional theory, and historical practice in a mixed capitalist system, unpublished doctoral dissertation, Cornell University, Ithaca, New York.

Rosenblum, S. (1980). "Swedish social democracy: At the crossroads." *Contemporary Crises, 4*, 267-282.

Ruggie, M. (1984). *The State and Working Women: Comparative Study of Britain and Sweden*. Princeton: Princeton University Press.

Rydén, B. (1967). "Concentration and structural adjustment in Swedish industry during the post-war period." *Skandinaviska Banken Quarterly Review,* No. 2, 51-58.

Rydén, B. (1972). *Mergers in Swedish Industry*. Stockholm: Almqvist & Wiksell.

SAF (1976). "Company profits, sources of investment capital and wage-earner funds." *SAF Document No. 1444*. Stockholm: SAF.

SAF (1981). "Collective wage-earner funds will harm Sweden." *SAF Document No.1442*. Stockholm: SAF.

SAF (1985). "Report on the wage-earner funds." *SAF Document No. 1449*. Stockholm: SAF.

Sainsbury, D. (1980). *Swedish Social Democratic Ideology and Electoral Politics 1944-1948*. Stockholm: Almqvist & Wiksell.

Sainsbury, D. (1981). "Theoretical perspectives in analyzing ideological change and persistence: The case of Swedish social democratic party ideology." *Scandinavian Political Studies, 4*, 273-294.

Samuelsson, K.S. (1957-58). "The banks and the financing of industry in Sweden, c. 1900-1927." *Scandinavian Economic History, 5-6*, 176-190.

Sandberg, L.G. (1978). "Banking and economic growth in Sweden before World War I." *Journal of Economic History, 38*, 650-680.

Scase, R. (1977). *Social Democracy in Capitalist Society: Working-Class Politics in Britain and Sweden.* London: Croom Helm.

Scott, F.D. (1988). *Sweden: The Nation's History.* Carbondale: Southern Illinois University Press.

Severin, F. (1956a). The ideological development of democratic socialism. *Socialist International Information, 6,* 215-248.

Severin, F. (1956b). *The ideological development of Swedish social democracy.* Stockholm: Tryckeriaktiebolaget Tiden.

Shalev, M. (1980). Socialism and the welfare state in democratic polities: The limits and possibilities of a class conflict interpretation. Paper presented at the Sapir Conference on Social Policy Evaluation, Tel-Aviv.

Shalev, M. (1983a). "Class politics and the Western welfare state." In Spiro, S.E. & Yuchtman-Yarr, E. (eds), *Evaluating the Welfare State: Social and Political Perspectives.* New York: Academic Press.

Shalev, M. (1983b). "The social democratic model and beyond: Two 'generations' of comparative research on the welfare state." *Comparative Social Research, 6,* 315-351.

Shearer, D., Rumberger, R., and Carnoy, M. (1983). *A New Social Contract: The Economy and Government After Reagan.* New York: Harper and Row.

Skandinaviska Enskilda Banken (n.d.). *Some Data About Sweden 1985-1986.* Stockholm: Skandinaviska Enskilda Banken.

Skocpol, T. and Amenta, E. (1986). "States and social policies." *American Review of Sociology, 12,* 131-157.

Skogh, G. (1984). "Employers associations in Sweden." In J.P. Windmuller and A. Gladstone (eds), *Employers Associations and Industrial Relations: A Comparative Study.* Oxford: Clarendon Press.

Skole, R. (1987). "The world of the Wallenbergs." *Sweden Now, 21,* 60-63.

SOU (1983:17). *Naringspolitiska effekter av internationella investeringar.* Stockholm: Statens offentliga utrediningar, Industriedepartementet.

Ståhl, I. (1977). "The expansion of the public sector." *SAF Document No. 1095.* Stockholm: SAF.

Steinmo, S. (1988). "Social democracy vs. socialsim: Goal adaptation in social democratic Sweden." *Politics and Society, 16,* 403-446.

Stephens, E.H. and Stephens, J.D. (1982). "The labor movement, political power, and workers' participation in Western Europe." *Political Power and Social Theory, 3,* 215-249.

Stephens, J.D. (1976). The consequences of social structural change for the development of socialism in Sweden. Unpublished doctoral dissertation, Yale University.

Stephens, J.D. (May 3-9, 1978). "Swedish social democracy heads beyond welfare state." *In These Times, 24*, 7-8.
Stephens, J.D. (1979). "Class formation and class consciousness: A theoretical and empirical analysis with reference to Britain and Sweden." *British Journal of Sociology, 30*, 389-414.
Stephens, J.D. (1980). *The Transition from Capitalism to Socialism.* New Jersey: Humanities Press.
Stephens, J.D. (1981a). "The changing Swedish electorate: Class voting, contextual effects, and voter volatility. *Comparative Political Studies, 14*, 163-204.
Stephens, J.D. (1981b). "The ideological development of the Swedish social democrats." In B. Denitch (ed.), *Democratic Socialism: The Mass Left in Advanced Industrial Societies.* Montclair: Allanheld, Osmun & Co.
Stephens, J.D. (1981c). "Impasse and Breakthrough - in Sweden." *Dissent, 28*, 308-318.
Street, J. (1983). "Socialist arguments for industrial democracy." *Economic and Industrial Democracy, 4*, 519-539.
Stuart, C.E. (1981). "Swedish Tax Rates, Labour Supply and Tax Revenues." *Journal of Political Economy, 5.*
Sundqvist, S. (1987). *Owners and Power in Sweden's Listed Companies.* Stockholm: Dagens Nyheter.
Svenska Bankföreningen (1987). *The Swedish Credit Market.* Stockholm: Graforama.
Svensson, L. (1986). "Class struggle in a welfare state in crisis: From radicalism to neoliberalism in Sweden." In R. Edwards, P. Garonna, and F. Todtling (eds), *Unions in Crisis and Beyond.* Dover, Mass.: Auburn House.
Sweden Now (1973:5). "Rank-and-file politics."
Sweden Now (1977:11). "A most multinational nation."
Swedenborg, B. (1979). *The Multinational Operations of Swedish Firms.* Stockholm: Almqvist & Wicksell.
Swedenborg, B. (1985). "Sweden." In J.H. Dunning (ed.), *Multinational Enterprises, Economic Structure and International Competitiveness.* Chichester: John Wiley & Sons.
Swedish Institute (1984). *Fact Sheets on Sweden: The Swedish Motor Industry.* Stockholm: Swedish Institute.
Swedish Institute (1986). *Fact Sheets on Sweden: The Swedish Economy.* Stockholm: Swedish Institute.
Swedish Ministry of Labour (1985). *The Swedish Act on Co-Determination at Work.* Stockholm: Ministry of Labour.

Swenson, P. (1989). *Fair Shares: Unions, Pay, and Politics in Sweden and West Germany.* Ithaca: Cornell University Press.
TCO (1987). *Presenting TCO.* Stockholm: TCO.
Therborn, G. (1969). "Swedish communism - End of an interlude." *New Left Review, 58,* 37-42.
Therborn, G. (1976). "The Swedish class struggle 1930-1965." In R. Scase (ed.), *Readings in the Swedish Class Structure.* Oxford: Pergamon Press.
Therborn, G. (1983). "Which class wins?" *New Left Review, 138,* 37-55.
Therborn, G. (1984a). "Classes and states: Welfare state developments, 1881-1981." *Studies in Political Economy, 14,* 7-41.
Therborn, G. (1984b). "The prospects of labour and the transformation of advanced capitalism." *New Left Review, 145,* 5-38.
Therborn, G. (1985). "The coming of Swedish social democracy." In E. Collotti (ed.), *L'Internazionale Operaia e Socialista tra le due Guerre.* Milan: Feltrinelli.
Therborn, G. (1986a). "Karl Marx returning: The welfare state and neo-Marxist, corporatist and statist theories." *International Political Science Review, 7,* 131-164.
Therborn, G. (1986b). *Why Some Peoples Are More Unemployed Than Others.* London: Verso.
Therborn, G. (1986c). "The working class and the welfare state." In P. Kettunen (ed.), *Det Nordiska i den Nordiska Arbetarorelsen.* Helsinki: Finnish Society for Labour History and Cultural Traditions.
Therborn, G. (1987). "Welfare states and capitalist markets." *Acta Sociologica, 30,* 237-254.
Therborn, G., Kjellberg, A., Marklund, S, and Öhlund, U. (1978). Sweden before and after social democracy: A first overview. *Acta Sociologica,* Supplement, 37-58.
Thunholm, L. (1981). "Commercial banks and industrial development." *Skandinaviska Enskilda Banken Quarterly Review, 1-2,* 3-11.
Tilton, T.A. (n.d.). *Nils Karleby: Socialist.* Stockholm: Arbetslivcentrum.
Tilton, T.A. (1979). "A Swedish road to socialism: Ernst Wigforss and the ideological foundations of Swedish social democracy." *American Political Science Review, 73,* 505-520.
Tilton, T.A. (1984). "Utopia, incrementalism, and Ernst Wigforss' conception of a provisional utopia." *Scandinavian Studies, 56,* 36-54.
Tilton, T.A. (1987). "Why don't the Swedish Social Democrats nationalize industry?" *Scandinavian Studies, 59,* 142-166.
Timashkova, O.K. (1978). *Scandinavian Social Democracy.* Moscow: Progress Publishers.

Tingsten, H. (1955). "Stability and vitality in Swedish democracy." *Political Quarterly, 26,* 140-150.

Tingsten, H. (1973). *The Swedish Social Democrats.* New Jersey: Bedminster Press.

Tomasson, R.F. (1973). Introduction. In H. Tingsten, *The Swedish Social Democrats.* New Jersey: Bedminster Press.

Törnblom, L. (1977). "The Swedish state company limited Statsföretag AB: Its role in the Swedish economy." *Annals of Public and Co-operative Economy, 48,* 451-461.

Uusitalo, H. (1979). "The working class: Still the grave-digger of capitalism?" *Acta Sociologica, 22,* 289-292.

Vahlne, J. (1983). "Foreign direct investments: A Swedish policy problem." In W.H. Goldberg (ed.), *Governments and Multinationals: The Policy of Control Versus Autonomy.* Cambridge, Mass.: Oelgeschlager, Gunn & Hain.

Vahlne, J. (1985). "International enterprise in Swedish industry." *Current Sweden,* No. 343.

Vanek, J. (1975). "Introduction." In J. Vanek (ed.), *Self-Management: Economic Liberation of Man.* Baltimore: Penguin Education.

Verney, D.V. (1959). *Public Enterprise in Sweden.* Liverpool: Liverpool University Press.

Von Otter, C. (1980). "Swedish Welfare Capitalism: The Role of the State." In R. Scase (ed.), *The State in Western Europe.* London: Croom Helm.

Westholm, C. (1977). "Should the free market economy be abolished?" *SAF Document No. 1095.* Stockholm: SAF.

Wheeler, C. (1975). *White-Collar Power: Changing Patterns of Interest Group Behavior in Sweden.* Urbana: University of Illinois Press.

Wigforss, E. (1924). "Industrial democracy in Sweden. *International Labour Review, 9,* 667-679.

Wilensky, H.L. (1976). *The New Corporatism, Centralization and the Welfare State.* Beverly Hills: Sage.

Wilensky, H.L. (1975). *The Welfare State and Equality.* Berkley: University of California Press.

Wolfe, A. (1978). "Has social democracy a future?" *Comparative Politics, 11,* 100-125.

Wolfe, D. (1983). "The Crisis in Advanced Capitalism: An Introduction." *Studies in Political Economy, 11,* 7-26.

Wolfe, D. (1989). "The Canadian state in comparative perspective." *Canadian Review of Sociology and Anthropology, 26,* 95-126.

Yunker, J.A. (1986). "Would democracy survive under market socialism?" *Polity, 18,* 678-695.

Zysman, J. (1983). *Governments, Markets and Growth: Financial Systems and the Politics of Industrial Change.* Ithaca: Cornell University Press.

Index

Adler-Karlson, G. 102, 103
Agrarian Party 54, 55, 57, 60, 61, 64, 98, 113, 117
 see also Centre Party
AP (pension funds) 64, 69
ATP (fourth pension fund) 32, 37, 38, 63, 70
 see also pension funds

Basic Agreement 9, 10, 87
 see also Saltsjöbaden Agreement
Bernstein, E. 3-6, 91, 94, 95, 99
Branting, H. 16, 95, 97

Cameron, D. 8
Centre Party 61, 67, 79, 83
co-determination 22, 28, 29, 30
Communist Party of Sweden
 see VPK

Conservative Party 18, 52-54, 63, 67, 79, 83, 101
 see also Moderate Party (Moderata Samlingspartiet)
corporatism 1, 120
"cow trade" (crisis agreement) of 1933 54

Dahl, R. 21, 41
December Compromise 15, 53
DGB (German trade union confederation) 12
Director's Club 55, 56, 87

Edin, P.O. 37
EFO model 10, 18, 66
employer associations 48
 see also SAF
 SHIO-Familjeföretagen
 SI, VF

Engels, F. 3
Erfurt Program 3, 6, 94, 99
Erlander, T. 98, 99
Esping-Andersen, G. 12
ESOPs (employee stock ownership plans) 32
European Community 65, 117, 118
Exchange Control Board 68, 75

Fabian 4, 6, 21, 61, 94
Feldt, K.O. 36, 105, 106, 119
folkhem (the people's home) 98, 102
Folkpartiet 79, 91
  see also Liberal Party
"Fourth of October" 81, 115, 116
"functional socialism" 100, 102, 104, 112

Gleitze, B. 12
Gleitze Plan 12
Gimle Program 94
Gotha Program 3, 94
Gothenburg Program 6, 20, 23, 99
Gourevitch, P. 52, 55, 88

Hansson, P.A. 97, 98
Hayek, F.A. 57
Hedborg, A. 11, 104
Hermansson, C.H. 65
Higgins, W. 26

Investeringsbanken (state-owned investment bank) 32
Investment Fund Reserve System (IF system) 88, 116
IUI (industry's research institute) 55, 56, 82

Jessop, B. 55

Karleby, N. 97-99, 102, 103, 104
Kautsky, K. 3, 4, 94
Korpi, W. 66, 106
Kreuger Empire 61, 87

Lasalle, F. 94
"legislative offensive" 26-31
Lenin, 3, 5
Lewin, L. 91-93
Liberal Party 18, 32, 54, 61, 63, 64, 67, 79, 83, 91
  see also Folkpartiet
Lindbeck, A. 82, 83
LKAB (Luosavaara-Kiirunavaara AB) 16, 101
LO (blue-collar confederation) 9, 11, 13-16, 18, 19, 26, 27, 32, 33, 35, 37, 52, 53, 58, 63, 74, 83, 91, 93, 96, 97, 100, 104-109, 111, 112, 115, 118
Luxemburg, R. 3-5, 7

market socialism 2, 17
Martin, A. 26
Marx, K. 3, 91, 92
Marxist 2, 7, 9, 14, 20, 91, 92, 94, 120
  see also neo-Marxist
MBL (Medbestämmendelagen) 28
Meidner, R. 10, 11, 13, 14, 17, 32, 104-106
Metallindustriarbetareförbundet (Metalworker's Union) 11, 58
Michels, R. 119
middle way 9, 11
Miliband, R. 7, 119
Moderate Party 79
  see also Conservative Party
Möller, G. 95, 97

Myrdal, G. 56, 97, 102

neo-Marxist 1, 2, 6, 7, 15, 43
"new factories" 25, 26
Nilsson, Å. 11

OECD (Organization for Economic Cooperation and Development) 8
Palm, A. 94
Palme, O. 27, 105
Pateman, C. 21
pension funds 63, 64, 70, 116
People's Home (folkhem) 98
PHM campaign ("Opposition to Economic Planning") 57, 81
Pontusson, J. 59, 86
post-war planning commission 55, 56
post-war planning program (the "27 point program") 55-57, 64, 100, 101
Poulantzas, N. 44
Procordia 41
Przeworksi, A. 102, 119, 120

reformism/reformist 1, 3-7, 9, 11
Rehn, G. 10, 42
Rehn-Meidner model/plan 9, 10, 33, 53, 58-60, 63, 68, 88, 100, 114
revisionism/revisionist 3, 4
revolution 3-5
Riksbank (central bank) 61, 62, 68, 69, 78
Riksdag (parliament) 61

SACO/SR (Swedish confederation of Professional associations/Federation of Civil Servants) 106, 107, 112, 114

SAF (Swedish employers' association) 9, 15, 18, 19, 24-26, 52-57, 67, 78-80, 83, 86, 117
Saltsjöbaden Agreement 9, 15, 24, 55
Sandler, R. 97, 99
SAP (Social Democratic Party of Sweden) 2, 6, 8-10, 13-15, 17, 20, 24, 27, 33, 35-37, 47, 48, 53-58, 60-64, 66-70, 79, 81, 83, 84, 90-93, 95-97, 100-102, 104-106, 108, 111-113, 116-120
SEB (Skandinaviska Enskilda Bank) 71
Second International 3, 6
SHIO-Familjeföretagen (Swedish Federation of Crafts and Medium-Sized Companies-Swedish Association of Family Enterprises) 79, 80
socio-technical changes 24-26
solidaristic wage policy 10, 11, 15, 22, 59, 74, 78, 104, 116, 118
SPD (Social Democratic Party of Germany) 6, 94
SI (Swedish association of industries) 52, 54, 55, 57, 79, 80
SIF (Swedish Union of Clerical and Technical Employees in Industry) 109-111
ST (Federation of Civil Servants) 109
Statsföretag (state holding company) 32, 41
see also Procordia
Sträng, G. 67

TCO (white-collar confederation)
  16, 27, 79, 91, 106-112, 114
third way 9, 11, 17, 18
Tilton, T. 113
Tingsten, H. 91-93

Undén, O. 98, 102
VF (association of engineering
  industries) 52, 54
VPK (Communist Party) 70, 97,
  100, 113, 117

Waldenström, E. 79
Waldenström Report 79, 80
Wallenberg, A.O. 50
Wallenberg empire 50, 52, 71, 73,
  80, 88, 89
Wigforss, E. 6, 16, 20, 23, 33, 56,
  97-99, 102, 104, 113